Children's Clothes
Easy to make clothes for 1-10 year olds

Written by Pamela Rodway
Illustrated by Laura Potter
Photography by Richard Sharpe Studios

ARCO PUBLISHING COMPANY, INC.
NEW YORK

Published 1975 by Arco Publishing Company, Inc.
219 Park Avenue South, New York, N.Y. 10003
  Designed and produced for
  Arco Publishing Company, Inc. by
  Intercontinental Book Productions.
Copyright © 1974 by Intercontinental Book Productions
All rights reserved
Library of Congress Catalog Card Number 74-19758

ISBN 0-668-03693-1

Printed in Spain

CONTENTS

1846231

INTRODUCTION

In order to make things as easy as possible we have arranged the book as follows:
Pages 7 to 13 have all sorts of sewing instructions. There's a full list and explanation of the sewing equipment you will need, a sizing and measuring chart so that you can check the exact size of your child (before beginning to make your patterns!), sewing instructions for stitches, sewing in zippers, setting in collars and sleeves, putting up hems, and so on. Perhaps most important of all, on page 8, there are full instructions for how to use the graph patterns given with each of the sewn garments. We would strongly recommend that you read *all of this section very carefully before* starting on any garment in the book. It contains lots of sound useful information pertaining specifically to this book.

Following this, on pages 14-73 are the patterns for the sewn garments for children. Fresh and unique designs, they will appeal as much to fashion conscious youngsters as to their parents. Follow our step-by-step instructions for making each garment and you should have no problems. If, however, this is your first sewing venture, do try one or two of the easier things first, the Mini-Pini, for example, on page 14, or for an older child, the skirts on pages 64-67. If you launch straight into the beautiful, tailored, and rather more complicated Fur Coat on page 40 without trying anything else first — you may just be a little disappointed with your results.

Remember to use suitable fabrics for the particular item you are making. For coats use coatweight fabric or your results will simply not be as pleasing. Similarly, buy zippers, buttons, bias bindings, sewing threads and any trimmings such as braid, that really match your fabric beautifully.

On pages 74-79 there are instructions for how to knit and crochet, along with notes on tension, pressing, sewing up and so on. Once again we do advise careful reading of these pages before starting on any of the lovely knitting patterns that begin on page 80 and go through to the end of the book. It is the final touches to knitted garments that can make them look professional!

In all cases the amount of material or yarn and the sewing requirements, such as number and size of buttons, length of zipper etc. are listed under the YOU WILL NEED heading. We have not included such things as pins, needles, sewing thread, sewing machine, scissors, and so on which you will need constantly.

W.S. and R.S. are frequently referred to in our instructions. They mean Wrong Side or sides of fabric, and Right Side or sides of fabric respectively. So R.S. together means 'place the right sides of both pieces of fabric together', prior to pinning, tacking or stitching. Where we have said 'stitch' in the instructions, it indicates machine stitching. 'Sew' means hand-sewing (type of stitch is usually stipulated).

SEWING INFORMATION

Before you begin to sew check through to make sure you have all the essential sewing equipment. You will need:

Dressmaker's graph paper, Ruler, Felt pen, Pencil and Cellophane tape — for making your paper patterns.

Pins — use the rustless kind. Glass-headed pins are particularly easy to use and show up well on most fabrics.

Needles—of various sizes so that you have fine needles for delicate fabrics, and thicker ones for woolens and so on. A package of assorted needles should provide you with all you need. You should also have a darning needle and a crewel needle.

Sewing Thread—you will need a selection of colors and thicknesses. Mercerized cotton is particularly good. In addition you should have a spool of tacking thread (soft and cheaper than sewing thread), cotton thread for thicker materials, and buttonhole twist for working buttonholes and loops.

Bodkin—helps in threading elastic through hemmed openings. Alternatively, you can use a safety pin.

Scissors—you need an ordinary pair of scissors for cutting out your paper patterns, a medium or large sharp pair of dressmaker's scissors for cutting out fabric and a small pair of sharp pointed scissors for cutting button-holes, clipping into curves etc.

Thimble—to fit on to the middle finger of your sewing hand.

Tape measure—those made of glass fiber with metal ends are the best as they do not stretch.

Iron and Ironing Board—keep close by and ready for use all the time you are sewing. You should be using them frequently!

Sewing Machine—most of the garments in the first section of this book were made with the use of a sewing machine. As explained on page 9 it is not possible to talk specifically about sewing machines as there are now so many different ones on the market. The important thing is to thoroughly read the handbook provided with your machine and practice all stitches extensively before using it to make garments.

There are other items of equipment that can make dress-making a little easier, but are not absolutely essential. These include:

Tailor's Chalk, or a Tracing Wheel and Dressmaker's Carbon Paper—for transferring details from patterns on to the fabric.

Unpicking Gadget—useful for unpicking rows of machine stitching when necessary.

A Sewing Gauge with a moveable marker—can be useful for checking the width of a hem as you turn it up.

Magnet—useful for picking up spilled-pins and clearing up after a sewing session.

Pinking Shears—as they cut with a serrated edge, they can be useful for neatening the edge of some materials. Not as efficient as neatening by hand or machine stitching.

Pincushion—for pins and needles.

Sleeveboard—useful for pressing around cuffs and armholes.

MEASUREMENT CHART

Age/Size	6 months	1 year	2 years	3 years	4 years	5 years	6 years	7 years	8 years
CHEST	ins. 19	ins. 20	ins. 21	ins. 22	ins. 23	ins. 24	ins. 25	ins. 26	ins. 27
WAIST	19	19½	20	20½	21	21½	22	23	23½
HIP	—	—	—	—	24	25	26	27	28
BACK NECK LENGTH	—	8¼	8½	9	9½	10	10½	11½	12
APPROX. HEIGHT	28	31	34	37	40	43	46	50	52

HOW TO TAKE MEASUREMENTS

CHEST	Take tape measure around fullest part of the chest.
WAIST	Take tape measure around the natural waistline.
HIP	Take tape measure around fullest part of the body below waist.
BACK NECK LENGTH	Take tape measure from the prominent bone at the back of neck to the waistline.

MAKING PAPER PATTERNS

All the patterns for the garments in this book are given as graph patterns, which means they must be made into paper patterns before they can be used. This is easily done by transferring them on to dressmaker's graph paper (available from sewing departments of large stores and fabric stores). The easiest way to make a paper pattern is as follows:

1. Check the scale on the graph pattern. Unless otherwise stated, 1 square on each of our patterns equals 3 inches, i.e. each square on our patterns equals 3 of the 1-inch squares, clearly marked on dressmaker's graph paper.

2. Number the squares on graph patterns across the top and down the sides. Number pattern paper in the same way, taping pieces together if necessary.

3. Draw all vertical and horizontal straight lines of pattern pieces first. Mark dots on lines of pattern paper to correspond with ends of curved lines on graph patterns.

4. Join up dots following curves of graph pattern. Erase and draw again if they are not correct. Transfer all words and markings on to your pattern as well.

5. Check the pattern pieces against the child to make sure they fit and make any alterations necessary at *this* stage. Then cut out the pattern pieces. If you feel you will use the pattern again, make a trace-off duplicate pattern, using the original as the master.

6. Place and carefully pin each pattern piece on to the fabric. Our graph patterns have been designed to show the correct way to fold the material and place the pattern pieces for the most economical use of fabric, so use them as a guide. Most pattern pieces need to be cut on double fabric as 2 pieces are needed for the garment.

Note that instructions are given with the patterns for making them a size smaller or larger, and that all graph patterns include $\frac{1}{2}$in. seam allowance.

When you have cut out the garment follow the sewing instructions, trying the garment on the child at anytime you are not sure of the fit. Pay particular attention to collars, sleeves and hemlines.

All the seams used in this book are plain or open seams, i.e. the 2 pieces of fabric placed right sides together and stitched down the seam line, which is $\frac{1}{2}$ in. from the raw edges. Press all seams at each stage of sewing and neaten them, either by oversewing (see page 9) or by turning under a tiny single hem (i.e. just one layer of material turned over) and stitching along this.

TACKING STITCH

Tacking is used to hold 2 pieces of material together prior to fitting or machining. It should be worked along the line where stitching will take place. All garments should be tacked together and tried on and fitted before machine stitching is commenced.

To tack, thread needle with a long piece of thread and knot one end. Make even stitches $\frac{1}{2}$in. long parallel with the edge through both thicknesses of fabric. Fasten end by taking 2 stitches back through the material.

RUNNING STITCH

Running is worked in the same way as tackling except the stitches should be $\frac{1}{8}$ in. long. 4 or more stitches can be taken before the needle is drawn away from the work. Running stitch is used when gathering is required-such as around sleeve heads or tops of skirts.

TAILOR TACKS

This is a quick way of marking pattern outlines or details such as darts or pleats.

1. Use a really long thread of double tacking cotton and then tack in the usual way—see Tacking Stitch—but leave each stitch quite loose so that it lies in a loop on the surface.

2. When tacking is complete, gently pull the two thicknesses apart as far as the loops will extend—usually about $\frac{1}{2}$in. Cut the stitches apart between the two surfaces, and each will be found to be marked accurately with the short ends of thread.

You can also use tailor's chalk or a tracing wheel to mark pattern details on fabric.

BACK STITCH

All hand sewing should begin and end with 1 or 2 back stitches in order to secure the thread. It is very firm stitching and can be used for joining fabric together instead of machine stitching.

Thread needle and knot thread. Working from right to left, bring needle through fabric from back and put back into material $\frac{1}{8}$in. *back* from where it came through. Bring it out $\frac{1}{8}$in. in front. Put back into fabric at end of previous stitch and bring out a stitch length in front. Repeat along line.

OVERSEWING

This is a method of neatening a plain seam after it has been opened and pressed flat. It can also be used to join 2 edges of material together.

Starting from the underside of the fabric, working from left to right, put your needle in the cloth $\frac{1}{4}$in. from the edge. Pull through, allowing the thread to loop over the raw edge of the cloth. Repeat this but $\frac{1}{4}$in. further along the raw edge. Continue until the raw edge is neatened.

HERRINGBONE STITCH

This is often used as a decorative stitch but can also be used to secure one piece of fabric to another firmly—but very neatly.

Work from left to right. Use two parallel lines to guide the stitches. Bring the needle through from the wrong side at one end of the upper line. Take the thread forward and downward to the lower line, then pick up a small horizontal stitch with the needle pointing backwards.

Pull through, take the needle diagonally upwards and forwards to the upper line and make another backward stitch there. (Needle should come out level with the beginning of the preceding stitch—see diagram.) Continue stitching alternatively on the two lines, so that a kind of cross stitch is formed.

MACHINE STITCHING

Make sure you understand how to use your machine before attempting any sewing of garments. Practice all the stitches and tensions on scraps of fabric.

The instruction book of your machine will give you all the details of threads and needles. It is not possible to give them all here as manufacturers' instructions vary.

Many machines have useful attachments. Learn how to use them all as most of them will save you time when stitching garments.

HEMS

1. PLAIN HEM—SLIPSTITCH

This is used when the fabric is thin and the garment a simple shape with no surplus fullness at the hemline. Fold fabric $\frac{1}{2}$in. from the raw edge to W.S. Then make a further turning. (The size of this turning should be about 2in. If more has to be turned to make the garment the right depth, cut off surplus.) Pin and tack fabric in place. This is the actual hemline of the garment. Thread the needle and, at the first fold line, working from right to left, insert the needle and pull through. $\frac{1}{4}$—$\frac{1}{2}$ in. along and insert the needle into the fold line again. Continue slip-stitching making sure the stitches are not pulled too tightly or they will show on the right side of the garment. Finish by taking a small stitch back through the material and out through the fold.

2. FLARED OR GATHERED HEM

This is used for turning up a bottom edge which is flared, bell-shaped or very definitely curved. In such cases the raw edge is distinctly wider than the part to which it is hemmed. The fullness of the hem can be dealt with in various ways Either run a gathering thread around hem $\frac{3}{4}$in. from raw edge and pull up to 'fit the skirt.' The hem should be as flat as possible. Alternatively, make tiny darts, tucks or pleats at regular intervals around the hem to dispose of fullness.

When the hem fits the skirt, stitch skirt tape or binding to the edge and hem this down onto the garment. Skirt tape is a flat tape and is used to avoid the bulky line which would result from turning the raw edge of the fabric inside and hemming.

WORKING A BUTTONHOLE

When making a row of buttonholes mark each one carefully before starting. Make sure they lie directly under one another at even distances apart.

1. Mark your buttonhole in pencil or tailor's chalk.

2. Sew a small running stitch, through the two thicknesses all around the buttonhole mark. This is to stop it fraying when it is cut.

3. Cut the buttonhole.

4. Work buttonhole stitch all around the raw edges as follows:
To start make a straight upward stitch the depth required (usually $\frac{1}{8}$in.).
Put the needle through to the wrong side at the end of this stitch bringing it up again on the raw edge of the button-hole slit, where it originally came from.
Make a second upright stitch, this time downwards towards the raw edge, holding the thread down with the left thumb so that it is under the needle. Pull up the needle. Pull up the thread, and it will form a base along the raw edge, known as the 'purl.' Continue to take upright stitches, bringing the needle back to the raw edge each stitch touching the previous stitch. Always keep the thread under the needle. When turning a corner, make a diagonal stitch going, at its inner end, into the same hole as the last upright stitch, and take the first upright stitch on the new line also into this hole; this gives a symmetrical effect.

WORKED LOOPS

Used at the edges of some garments for fastening buttons. Sew 3 or 4 strands through folded edge of material leaving them loose to the depth of the intended loop. Work buttonhole stitch over all threads right round the loop.

CROSSWAY OR BIAS STRIPS

Crossway or bias strips are usually used to bind curved edges. As they are cut diagonally across the fabric, on the true bias, they can be slightly stretched, without distorting, to fit neatly round curves.

1. Cut strips of required width at 45° angle to the straight edges of fabric. Do this by folding fabric diagonally so the crosswise grain is parallel to the lengthwise grain.

2. Place 'A' and 'B', right sides together and stitich.

3. Press open and trim away points that extend over the edges. You have a straight 'stretchy' strip with a diagonal seam.
Bought bias binding is also available and is particularly useful when you have insufficient fabric to cut crossway strips.

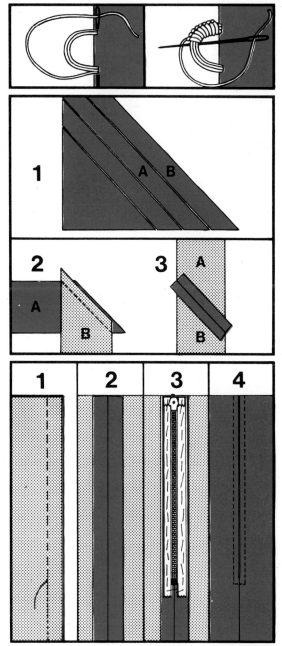

INSERTING A ZIPPER

1. Insert zipper after you have machine stitched the seam and neatened the edges. Right sides of fabric together, tack 2 sides of zipper opening together, continuing in a straight line from the machine stitching, and using small stitches.

2. Press fabric open.

3. Lay zipper against centre of tacked seamline, and tack into position.

4. On right side of garment machine stitch close to the zipper. (You will achieve best results by using the zipper foot, available for most sewing machines.) Remove seam tacking and your zipper will remain perfectly concealed.

SETTING A COLLAR

Make up the collar by placing right sides top collar and undercollar together, (interfacing tacked to W.S. of under collar, if needed) then tacking and machine stitching together leaving the neck edge unstitched. Trim turnings and turn collar to right side. Press.
To set the collar onto garment, mark the exact back center of the neckline on the garment with a pin and that of the underside of the collar with another.
Match the two pins and tack from them each way to the

collar fronts, the under collar resting on the right side of the garment. Do not tack the upper collar. Try on the garment, and make sure the collar is central. Machine stitch in place. Turn under the raw edge of the top collar and slip-stitch in place over raw edges of garment's collar.

SETTING IN A SLEEVE

Stitch the underarm seam on the sleeve and press. Run a gathering thread round the head of the sleeve $\frac{1}{2}$in. from the edge. Make sure you have the correct sleeve for the correct armhole.

Hold the garment with its wrong side towards you and the armhole well opened.

With the sleeve right side out, draw it through the armhole so that the edges of the sleeve and the armhole are level and you look into the wrong side of the sleeve. (Garment and sleeve are right side together).

Match the center of the sleeve to the shoulder seam of the garment. Pin the lower part of the sleeve and armhole together matching seams. Adjust the gathers of the upper sleeve part so that grain of the fabric hangs vertically down the sleeve. Pin the upper part of the armhole. Tack over the pins (see sketch) adjusting gathers. If it is a plain sleeve there should be a hardly noticeable fullness. Remove the pins and try the garment on the child. If it is comfortable and hangs well, stitch it in. If not, adjust, pin and re-tack.

DARTS

Some of the patterns in this book have darts incorporated in them, which help in shaping the garment. To work these, mark the lines of the dart from the pattern using tailor's tacks, chalk or a tracing wheel. Fold fabric along center of dart, R.S. inside and pin and tack in place. Machine stitch from the widest end towards the fold, so that the last few stitches come on the fold. Press the dart flat and then press it to one side.

FACINGS

Raw edges must always be neatened when making garments and 'facings' are often used in such places as neck, sleeve, front opening, and pocket edges. Facings are usually cut as a separate pattern piece and have been clearly shown on the graph patterns. Instructions for applying them are given in the individual sewing instructions.

Curved edges on garments such as around sleeve, necklines, trouser crotch seams etc. must be 'clipped' so they lie flat. To do this take small snips at approximate $\frac{1}{2}$—1 in. intervals from the edge of the fabric down to the stitched seam line. Press seam flat.

SMOCKING

The preliminary gathering of smocking is extremely important to the finished appearance — so it should be carefully and unhurriedly done. The dots can be marked at $\frac{1}{2}$in. or less intervals and on 2 to 4 times the required finished width of the smocking. Because of the concetration of the fabric, it is usually done on lightweight fabric.

1. Lay the material flat and pin, or tack it to tissue paper so that it does not move when you start marking it.

2. Using a ruler mark every $\frac{1}{2}$in. along and each row 1in. apart with a pencil.

3. Tack, taking the needle in and out of consecutive dots. Make sure stitches fall directly under each other in all lines.

4. When you have completed all rows, draw up the gathers and arrange them evenly. You can use a pin at the end of each row to secure the surplus thread. The gathered measurement should be one-third of the original length.

There are many embroidery stitches suitable for smocking, most of which are quite simple to do and look extremely attractive. The one used on the Long Party Dress on page 68 is called 'Honeycomb' and we give instructions for it on this page.

1. Thread the needle with embroidery thread and bring through the fabric from the wrong side at the left pleat of the second row.

2. Sew a back stitch which catches together the next pleat to the first one, in the same row, and the first one itself.

3. Sew another back stitch below the first one and then insert the needle into the second of the two pleats. Carry the needle up inside the pleat, so that it does not show, to the row immediately above.

4. As before, back stitch this pleat to the next. (This is the third pleat from the left as the stitch was started on the second.)

5. This time put the needle downwards inside the third pleat, taking it down to the lower row. Continue in this way, back-stitching together two pleats alternately in the lower and upper rows, the second pleat in one stitch always becoming the first in the next, so that a diamond pattern is formed.

Mini-Pini Cover-Up

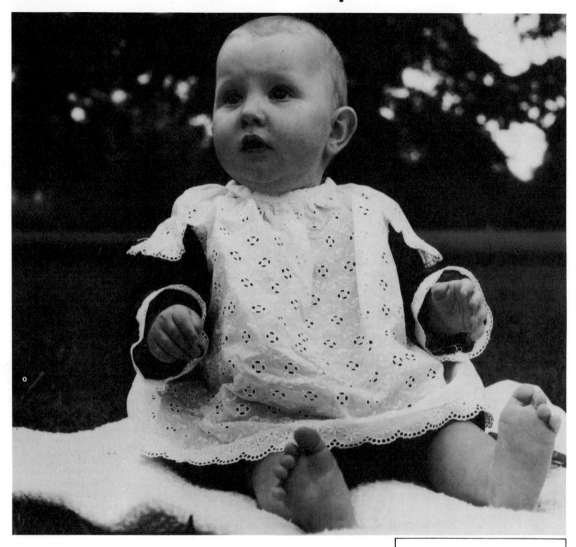

This pretty little smock cover-up could be made in toweling or plastic and so double as a bib. We chose crisp broderie anglaise — and the little dress worn underneath was made using the pattern for a christening gown on the next page.

TO ADJUST YOUR PATTERN:
Pattern is Size 1.
For one size larger lengthen by 1 in.
For a smaller size reduce by 1 in.

YOU WILL NEED

$\frac{1}{2}$ yd 34 in/35 in. wide broderie anglaise
Matching sewing thread
$2\frac{1}{2}$ yds edging lace

Cut out shapes shown for the armholes. Neaten the underarm (i.e. lower half of crescent shape).

PATTERN FOR MINI-PINI			NECK	TIE		
Each square = 3 inches						
		Cut-out for armhole				

SELVEDGES

FOLD

Gather lace to fit top armhole crescent shape and stitch in place. Press seam towards neck, and stitch around the curve. Run a gathering thread around lace, pull up and sew around the hem, pressing and top stitching in the same way.

Run a gathering thread around neck edge and pull up to required size — (measure child's neck and add $1\frac{1}{2}$ in.)

Divide neck tie in half. Place RS center front of neck tie to RS center front of cover-up. Pin one side of neck tie to neck edge adjusting gathers evenly. Pin other side.

Tack into position. Then fold in raw edges of the remainder of ties either side of the neck. Tack.

Fold over to cover raw edge of the binding on the neck. Tack. Stitch carefully through the whole length of the neck tie. Press.

Christening Gown

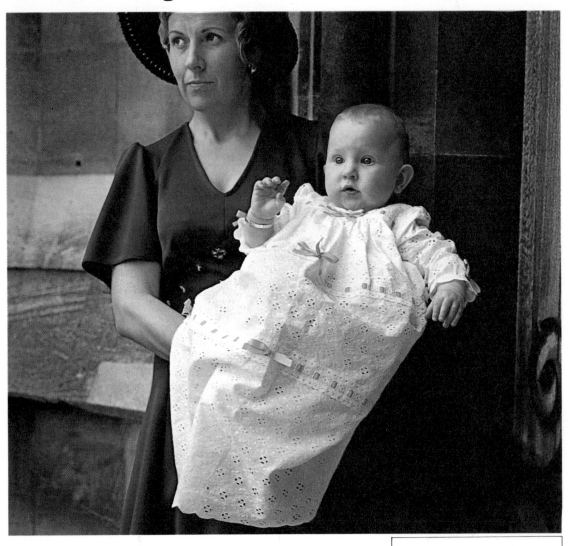

This enchanting pattern for a christening gown is for a six-month old baby. Enlarge the pattern as instructed overleaf to make a child's dress for a one year old baby.

YOU WILL NEED:

1⅓ yds 34 in./35 in. wide
   Broderie Anglaise
   flouncing
Matching Sewing Thread
Shirring elastic
Broderie Anglaise trim:
   approx 4 yds double-edged
   with ribbon slotting:
   approx ½ yd edging
4 yds narrow satin ribbon
12 make-up satin ribbon
   bows
3⅜ in. buttons, or smaller if
   preferred.

R.S. of body pieces together, pin, tack and stitch shoulder seams.

R.S. of skirt pieces together, pin, tack and stitch side seams.

Cut the slit for the back opening in the skirt. Turn edges to W.S. and slip stitch to neaten.

Run a gathering thread around top of skirt and draw up to fit bodice. Bodice back has an allowance for buttons and button-holes, so turn back on the marked line.

R.S. together, tack and stitch skirt to bodice, overlapping center of back bodice yoke. Thread satin ribbon through lace.

Sew lace on to dress. Positions for the double-edged lace are: approx. one-third of skirt length down from bodice yoke seam; halfway between this and the hem; and over the bodice/skirt seam (only a small amount should cover the skirt).

7

Stitch lace down center of sleeves to the wrist, stopping at elastication level.

8

Gather broderie anglaise edging and sew around neck. Cut a cross-way strip $1\frac{1}{4}$ in. x $10\frac{1}{2}$ in. and stitch to R.S. neck edge. Turn over to cover the raw edges and slip stitch into position.

9

Wind shirring elastic onto the bobbin of your machine following machine manufacturer's instructions. Stitch two rows $\frac{1}{4}$ in. apart along marked lines at wrist level on sleeves. Tie the ends of shirring elastic very securely.

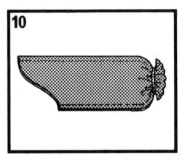

10

R.S. insides, tack and stitch sleeve seam.

11

Using running stitch, sew gathering thread around sleeve head and draw up to fit armhole. With R.S. of sleeve to R.S. garment, pin, tack and stitch in place (see page 12).

12

Make machine or hand-worked buttonholes at back yoke of garment (see page 11). Sew on buttons.

13

With small slip stitches, sew the made-up satin ribbon bows on to the gown.

FOLD

FRONT YOKE

SKIRT

BACK YOKE

button and buttonhole position

cut opening in back skirt only

(top)

cutting line for baby dress pattern

SELVEDGES

SELVEDGES

Elastication level

SLEEVE

(front)

(sleeve head)

PATTERN FOR CHRISTENING GOWN

Each square = 3 inches

TO ADJUST YOUR PATTERN:

To adapt the christening gown to make a size one baby dress shown at left, follow the enlarging instructions given on page 16. Cut the skirt below along the dotted line shown on the pattern.

To make baby dress pattern for size one you should make the following adjustments to your pattern:

FRONT YOKE: Extend yoke width by $\frac{1}{4}$ in.
                    Raise shoulder seam by $\frac{1}{4}$ in.

BACK YOKE: As front yoke

SLEEVE: Raise top point of sleeve by $\frac{1}{4}$ in. Extend width of sleeve at underarm point by $\frac{1}{4}$ in. Re-draw sleeve head connecting the new measurements. Lengthen bottom of sleeve by $1\frac{1}{8}$ in.

FRONT SKIRT: Extend skirt width by $\frac{1}{4}$ in.
                    Lengthen skirt 1 in.

BACK SKIRT: As front skirt.

For size two, extend your size one pattern by the same adjustments as above. To make up the garment as a baby dress, follow the instructions for making up the christening gown, but *omit* the double-edged lace application instructions on the sleeves and skirt. Add narrow lace edging to sleeves at the wrists.

The hem allowance on the pattern is $1\frac{1}{2}$ in.

19

Dungarees

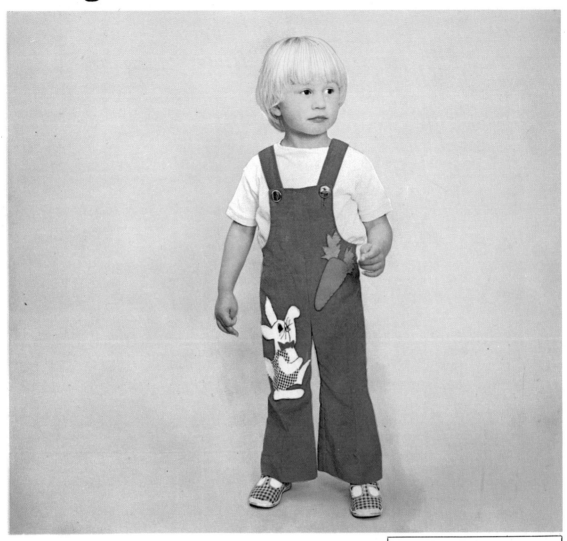

Make up these dungarees in plain material as we have and put on a motif, or use the same pattern and make up the dungarees in a check, stripe or any printed material.

TO ADJUST YOUR PATTERN:
The pattern is in Size 2.
Seam allowance is $\frac{1}{2}$ in.
Hem allowance on legs $1\frac{1}{4}$ in.
Back waist casing for elastic $1\frac{1}{4}$ in.

To make the pattern a size larger, adjust as follows:

FRONT: Keeping crotch point the same, extend length at top by $1\frac{1}{4}$ in. Widen by $\frac{1}{8}$ in. Extend length upwards at side seam by $\frac{1}{2}$ in. Redraw chest area connecting the new measurements. Widen dungaree at crotch level inside leg by $\frac{1}{4}$ in. Lengthen dungaree legs by 2 in.

BACK: Keeping crotch point the same, extend length at top by $\frac{1}{2}$ in. Widen dungarees at crotch level inside leg by $\frac{1}{4}$ in. Lengthen dungarees by 2 in.

STRAPS: Lengthen to desired measurement.
For a size smaller make similar adjustments but as reductions.

YOU WILL NEED
$1\frac{1}{2}$ yds 36 in. wide material.
Matching Sewing thread.
Buttonhole Twist.
2 $\frac{3}{4}$ in. buttons.
Scraps of White, Orange, Green and Red fabric for motif
Small amount of black and white material for the rabbit's trousers
Embroidery thread.
Elastic $\frac{1}{2}$ in. wide.

Turn seam allowance to W.S. on arm curve of dungaree front. Machine or slipstitch into position.

R.S. front and back pieces together, stitch side seams by machine from hem, upwards. The surplus material at the top of the dungaree back will be folded over later.

R.S. together, pin, tack and stitch front leg to back leg at inside leg seams.

Place one leg inside other with R.S. together. Pin, matching inside leg seams at crotch. Tack and stitch. Clip curved seams.

Turn $1\frac{1}{2}$ in. hem at top back to W.S. Slip stitch. Thread elastic through. Stitch one end; adjust to child's size and sew down end.

Turn seam allowance of $1\frac{1}{4}$ in. on front piece to W.S. for the top of the dungaree. Work buttonholes at each corner, either by machine or hand.

R.S. inside, stitch down length of straps. Turn through to R.S. Press. Turn in raw edges at ends and slip-stitch along openings.

8

Sew straps to back of dungarees, at an angle to allow them to cross at the center of the child's back. Turn under the excess material at end of straps as shown above, and slip stitch to W.S. top of dungarees to neaten.

9

Sew buttons on straps in position to correspond with the buttonholes, giving sufficient length of strap to allow the child to move comfortably.

10

Turn up pants leg hems to W.S. to fit child. Slip-stitch into position.

PATTERN FOR DUNGAREES   Each square = 3 inches

BACK

(side seam)

buttonhole

SELVEDGES

FOLD

FRONT

(side seam)

STRAPS

PATTERN FOR MOTIF   NB — each square = **2 in.**

1 Motif: Cut out rabbit completely in white fabric.

2 Cut out pants in black and white check, turn under raw edges and slip-stitch to rabbit shape.

5 Turn raw edges around rabbit under and slip stitch in required position on right-hand side of dungarees.

3 Outline eyes, nose and teeth in embroidery thread. Sew whiskers. Fill in eyes with small stitches.

4 Cut out red bow tie; turn raw edges under and slip stitch to rabbit.

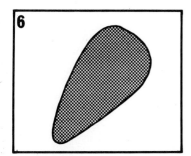

6 Cut out carrot shape from orange fabric.

8 Turn under raw edges of both shapes. Slip stitch to dungarees so that carrot slightly overlaps carrot top.

7 Cut out carrot-top shape from green fabric.

Shorts and a Jerkin

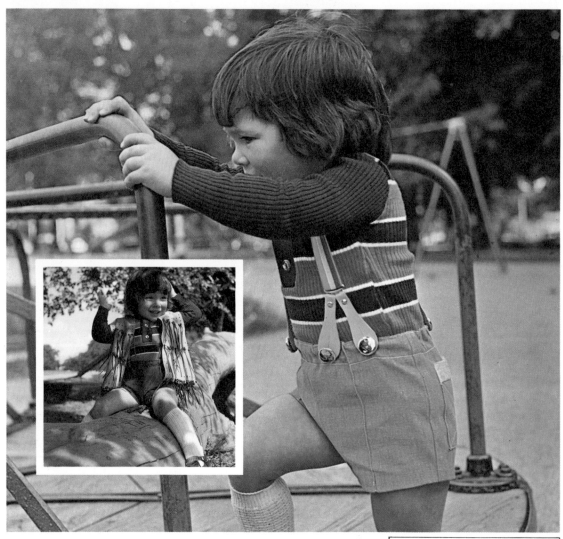

Make up these shorts in denim or imitation suede as we have done. The jerkin is in real suede and makes a neat top for an older brother. Follow the instructions to make it smaller, so it teams up with the shorts.

TO ADJUST YOUR PATTERN:

Shorts
The pattern is in Size 4.
To make the pattern a size larger adjust as follows:
FRONT: Add $\frac{1}{2}$ in. to top of shorts. Add $\frac{1}{8}$ in. to all other seams.
BACK: Make similar adjustments as front.
POCKETS AND POCKET FACINGS: Add $\frac{1}{8}$ in. to all seams.
For a size smaller make similar adjustments but as reductions.

Suede Jerkin
The pattern is Size 6.
For a size smaller make the following adjustments.
SHOULDER SEAM: Decrease length by $\frac{1}{8}$ in.
ARMHOLE: Fill in $\frac{1}{2}$ in. at underarm level, so armhole is smaller.
WIDTH: Decrease by 1 in.
LENGTH: Decrease by 1 in.
For a size larger, make similar adjustments but as enlargements.

YOU WILL NEED:
For the Shorts:
$\frac{1}{2}$ yd. of 36 in. wide fabric
Matching sewing thread
$\frac{1}{2}$ in. wide elastic
Purchased suspenders
Buttons (optional)

For the Jerkin:
1 suede skin 30 in. long
Matching sewing thread
Suede strips for thonging
Leather hole punch

Denim shorts:
Place W.S. of pocket facing to R.S. of pocket and stitch seam. (Reverse side of fabric is used as a trim.)

Turn top of facing under on fold line. Turn ½ in. of raw edges of pocket to W.S. and tack.

Machine stitch diagonal lines from corners on pocket, beneath facing trim.

Pin, tack and stitch pockets to R.S. back of shorts in required positions.

With R.S. together, pin, tack and stitch side seams.

R.S. together pin, tack and stitch front leg of shorts to back leg of shorts at inside leg seam.

Place one leg inside other with R.S. together. Pin, matching inside leg seams at crotch. Tack and stitch from front to back.

Clip seams at curves so they lie flat. Turn up 1 in. to W.S. on legs, hem and slip stitch into position.

PATTERN FOR SHORTS

Each square = 3 inches

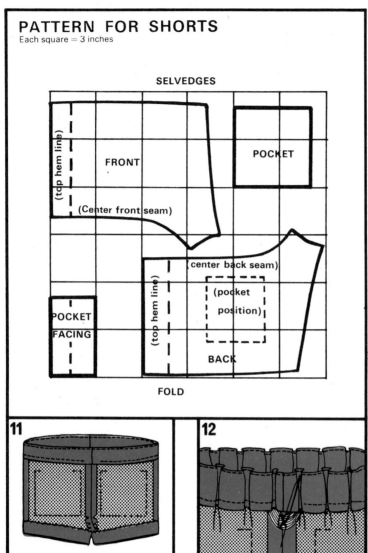

SELVEDGES

FRONT

POCKET

(top hem line)

(Center front seam)

(center back seam)

(pocket position)

POCKET FACING

(top hem line)

BACK

FOLD

9

Fold on front crease line and top stitch a row of machine stitching along crease.

10

Turn $1\frac{1}{2}$ in. at top of shorts to W.S. and topstitch a row of machine stitching at outer edge.

11

Turn raw edges under and stitch parallel line 1 in. from top, leaving small opening to insert elastic.

12

Insert elastic and adjust to required waist size. Sew ends together securely by hand. Slip stitch opening.

13

If the purchased suspenders button on to the shorts, sew buttons in required positions.

14

SUEDE SHORTS: Pocket facings are not required and it is not necessary to turn under raw edges as suede does not fray. Place pockets in required position on back of shorts and stitch without turning under edges.

15

Proceed as for denim shorts. (There is no need to turn up and hem bottom edge, but this can be done to give a finished look.)

1

SUEDE JERKIN: Carefully cut suede skin in half and lay out as shown. Cut out pattern pieces using sharp scissors.

2

Overlap one back seam over other and stitch two rows.

PATTERN FOR SUEDE JERKIN
Each square = 3 inches

(Center back)

(front edge)

CUT THE SUEDE SKIN IN HALF AND PLACE RIGHT SIDES TOGETHER, MAKING SURE THE GRAIN IS RUNNING THE SAME WAY ON EACH SKIN.

3

Punch holes $\frac{1}{2}$ in. apart at approximately these measurements *up* from the bottom. *1st Row:* $\frac{1}{2}$ in. *2nd Row:* 1 in. *3rd Row:* $5\frac{1}{2}$ in. *4th Row:* $6\frac{1}{2}$ in. *5th Row:* $9\frac{1}{2}$ in. *6th Row:* $10\frac{1}{2}$ in. 1st, 3rd and 5th rows are for thonging, the others for decoration only.

4

Punch holes $\frac{1}{2}$ in. from edge and $\frac{1}{2}$ in. apart around neck, fronts and armholes, omitting shoulder seams.

5

Cut thonging into 9 in. lengths. Thread through one hole and out through next. Tie a double knot. Repeat on 'thonging rows.'

6

Overlap front shoulders onto back shoulders. Sew two rows of stitching.

27

Play Jumper and Blouse

This bright little pinafore dress is very easy to make as it involves no machine stitching — all seams are glued together. The peasant blouse is easy to make too and can be worn just as effectively with pants or skirts.

TO ADJUST YOUR PATTERNS:

Pinafore
The pattern is in size 4
No hem allowance as felt does not fray.
To make the pattern a size larger adjust as follows:
FRONT: Extend from neck edge, shoulder seam and armhole lines by $\frac{1}{4}$ in.
                Widen side seams by $\frac{1}{4}$ in.
                Place center front $\frac{1}{8}$ in. from fold.
                Lengthen pinafore by 2 in.
BACK: As for front.
For a size smaller make similar adjustments but as reductions.

YOU WILL NEED:

For the pinafore:
$\frac{3}{4}$ yd. 36 in. wide felt
Matching Sewing Thread
Glue
Assorted scraps of felt in
    bright colors
Buttons
Thick yarn for stitching
Braid for trim

For the blouse:
1 yd 36 in. wide fabric
Matching thread
$\frac{1}{4}$ in. wide elastic
6 snaps

Fold a 5 in. square of paper as in diagram and draw the shape shown.

Cut out shape. Open paper fully and draw around shape on felt to make large flowers. Cut out. Glue in position on pinafore front.

Refold shape and use as pattern piece for smaller flowers. Cut out shapes and glue to pinafore.

Cut out 2 in. circles for center of flowers. Glue to flowers and sew buttons around.

Using thick yarn, sew large back stitches for 'stems.' 'Cut out small leaf shapes and glue to pinafore. One end of the leaf should touch the 'stems.'

Take the front pinafore and overlap the back pinafore at shoulder seams by 1 in. Glue.

Do the same to the side seams.

Pin the braid trim ⅜ in. in from the edges. Sew into position with running or slip stitch.

PATTERN FOR PLAY PINAFORE

Each square = 3 inches

FOLD

BACK

SELVEDGE

SELVEDGE

FRONT

FOLD

1 PEASANT BLOUSE: R.S. together, pin, tack and stitch shoulder and side seams together.

2 Turn center back turning to W.S. on fold line (not center back line). Stitch down.

3 R.S. inside, fold neckband lengthwise. Stitch short ends. Turn to right side out.

4 R.S. together, pin, tack and stitch one edge to blouse neck from center back, around to center back.

5 Fold in small remaining part of turning at back and slip stitch at top.

6 Turn neckband edge under to cover raw edges at neck and slip stitch in place.

7 Turn up a $\frac{1}{2}$ in. hem around bottom of blouse and stitch in place.

8 R.S. inside, pin, tack and stitch sleeve seams. Run a gathering thread around each sleeve head.

PATTERN FOR BLOUSE-TOP

Each square = 3 inches

FOLD

FRONT

BACK

NECKBAND (cut one only)

(sleeve head)

SLEEVE

(front)

Center back line

(fold line)

SELVEDGES

9 Turn bottom of sleeves to W.S. on fold line. Stitch 2 rows $\frac{1}{2}$ in. apart 1 in. in from fold. Leave small opening.

10 Measure around child's upper arm and cut elastic 1 in. shorter. Thread through stitching around sleeve and sew ends together.

11 Sew opening where elastic was threaded.

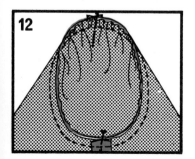

12 R.S. together, pin, tack and stitch sleeves to blouse adjusting gathers evenly around sleeve head.

13 Overlap right hand back on left. Sew 6 snaps on W.S. of right back and R.S. of left back to fasten blouse.

A Dress or a Smock

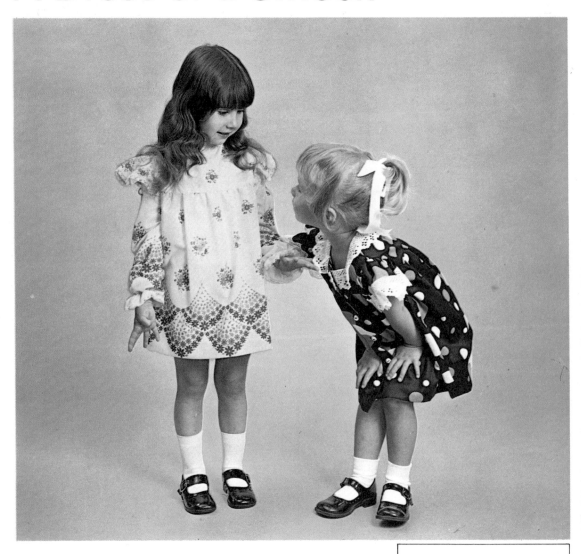

These great little dresses are both made from the same pattern. Make the smock from woolen material and it could team up with a turtleneck sweater on chilly days.

TO ADJUST YOUR PATTERN
The pattern is in Size 4.
To make a size larger adjust the pattern as follows:
FRONT: Widen pattern at armhole by $\frac{1}{4}$ in.
            Widen pattern at side seam by $\frac{1}{2}$ in.
            Adjust neck to required size.
            Lengthen skirt 2 in.
BACK: As for front.
SLEEVE: Widen sleeve by $\frac{1}{4}$ in. either side.
            Lengthen sleeve 1 in.
For a size smaller make similar adjustments but as reductions.

YOU WILL NEED:
for long sleeved dress:
$2\frac{1}{2}$ yds 36 in. wide fabric
Matching thread
Woven or neatened edge
    lace trimming
Buttons
Shirring elastic

for smock:
$1\frac{3}{4}$ yds 36 in. wide fabric
Matching thread
Woven or neatened edge
lace trimming
Buttons

1

R.S. together, pin, tack and stitch shoulder seams of yokes.

2

Run a gathering thread around back skirt. Pull up. R.S. together, pin, tack and stitch back skirt to back yoke.

3

Run a gathering thread around top of front skirts. Pull up and R.S. together, pin, tack and stitch to front yokes.

4

Fold fabric to W.S. along line at front for button and buttonhole allowance.

5

Pin and tack a crossway strip $12\frac{1}{2}$ in. x $1\frac{1}{2}$ in. around the neck. Stitch along one edge. Turn over to inside and slip stitch to cover raw edges.

6

R.S. together, pin, tack and stitch side seams.

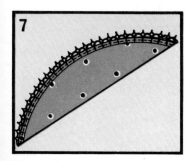

7

Turn under a small hem around bottom of sleeve frills. Stitch lace trimming to R.S. of sleeve close to edge.

8

Run a gathering thread around top of sleeve frills. R.S. together, tack into armhole. (Sleeve frills stop at yoke level.)

9

R.S. inside, pin, tack and stitch sleeve seam.

SELVEDGES

(fold line)

cutting line for square necked smock

(sleeve head)

SLEEVE FRILL

FRONT YOKE

BACK YOKE

(sleeve head)

(front)

SLEEVE

(top)

FRONT SKIRT

(top)

BACK SKIRT

FOLD

elastication level

10

11

12

Gather sleeve head. R.S. together, tack into armhole. Stitch through sleeve and sleeve frill around armhole.

Stitch lace around sleeve hem and around neck.

Thread machine with shirring elastic and stitch 2 rows around cuffs.

13 Turn up hem around bottom to fit child and slipstitch into position.

14 Make buttonholes by hand or by machine (see page 10). Sew on buttons, to correspond with these.

1 SMOCK: Cut along dotted lines on yoke patterns to make square neck for smocks. Cut out the yoke fronts and back on double fabric.

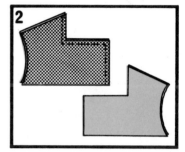

2 R.S. together, stitch around neck. Clip into corners (so neck is square and lies flat). Turn to R.S. and press.

3 Proceed as for dress but turn under and slip stitch small hems on lower armholes (necessary as sleeves are omitted).

4 Trim with lace as shown.

A Coat for Indoors or Out

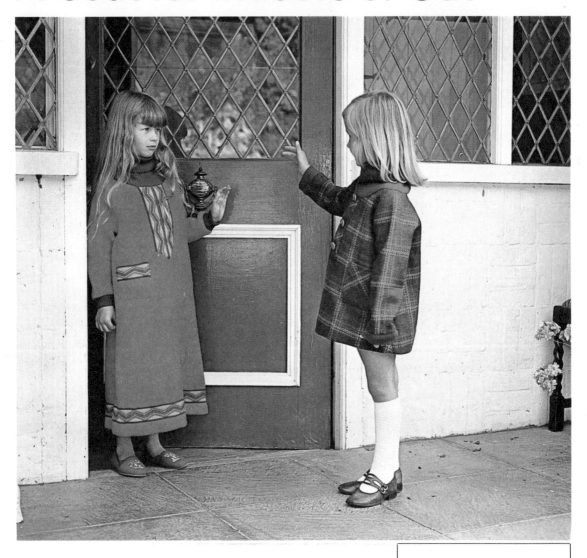

This attractive little outdoor coat can be lengthened and made into a warm wool housecoat.

TO ADJUST YOUR PATTERN:
Pull-on-Coat
The pattern is in size 4.
To make the pattern a size larger adjust as follows:

FRONT: Widen pattern at armholes by $\frac{1}{4}$ in.
               Widen pattern at side seam by $\frac{1}{4}$ in.
               Lengthen coat by 2 in.
BACK: As for front.
SLEEVE: Widen sleeves by $\frac{1}{4}$ in. at either side at underarm seam.
               Lengthen sleeves by 1 in.
BUTTON
STRAP: Increase width by $\frac{1}{8}$ in. and lengthen by 1 in.
POCKETS: Increase by $\frac{1}{8}$ in. all around.
For a size smaller make the same adjustments but as reductions.

YOU WILL NEED:
for coat:
$1\frac{1}{4}$ yds 54 in. wide material
Matching sewing thread
$3\frac{3}{4}$ in. buttons
Purchased knitted ribbing

for housecoat:
2 yds 54 in. wide material
Matching sewing thread
Contrasting braid trim
Purchased knitted ribbing

PULL-ON-COAT: R.S. together, pin, tack and stitch side seams.

R.S. inside, pin, tack and stitch sleeve seams.

With sleeve seam matching underarm seam, R.S. together, pin, tack and stitch sleeves into coat.

Turn up hem on coat to fit child and slip stitch into position

Turn ½ in. to W.S. all around button strap, and tack in place. Tack and slip stitch strap in position in center of coat.

Pockets — turn to W.S. on fold line at top. Press. Turn ½ in. to W.S. on all remaining raw edges. Pin, tack and stitch into position.

POCKET

SLEEVE

FRONT STRAP
(cut one only)

(sleeve head)

(front)

BACK

FRONT

PATTERN FOR COAT

FOLD

Each square = 3 inches

7 Cut purchased ribbing into one piece 13 in. × 11 in. for the neck and two pieces 4 in. × 4 in. for the cuffs.

8 Backstitch the two 11 in. sides together to make a tube and turn so stitching is on inside.

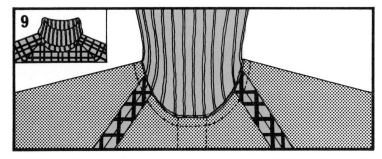

9 R.S. together, sew one end to raw neck edge of coat. Fold over free end to make collar.

10 Sew cuff ribs into a tube in the same way. Fold and stitch raw edge to R.S. of coat at cuff edge.

11 Sew buttons in position on button strap.

1 HOUSECOAT: Increase length of pattern to fit child's full length. Cut out pieces, omitting button strap and 1 pocket.

2 Make up as for coat. Stitch patterned braid down front instead of button strap.

3 Attach one pocket only in the same way as coat. Stitch braid in place on top of pocket and around hem.

Fun Fur Coat and Hat

Make this luxurious coat for your child in any fur fabric. We chose ocelot for ours but others would be just as effective. The saucy little hat completes a perfect outfit.

TO ADJUST YOUR PATTERN:
The pattern is in Size 5.
To make the pattern a size larger:

BACK: Increase neck length by $\frac{1}{16}$ in. (in total). Increase shoulder seam length by $\frac{1}{8}$ in. Increase side seam width by $\frac{1}{8}$ in. Increase coat length by 2 in. Re-draw the armhole.

FRONT: Increase neck length by $\frac{1}{16}$ in. (in total). Increase shoulder seam length by $\frac{1}{8}$ in. Increase side seam width by $\frac{3}{8}$ in. Increase coat length by 2 in. Re-draw the armhole.

SLEEVES: UPPER SLEEVE: Widen sleeve by $\frac{1}{8}$ in. either side. Lengthen sleeve by $\frac{3}{4}$ in. Re-draw sleeve head.
UNDER SLEEVE: Widen sleeve by $\frac{1}{16}$ in. either side. Lengthen sleeve by $\frac{3}{4}$ in. Re-draw underarm seam line.

COLLAR: Increase neck seam length by $\frac{1}{8}$ in. in total. Increase width of collar by $\frac{1}{16}$ in.

FACINGS: Re-draw front and back facings and interfacings to fit your new pattern.

For coat size 4, decrease by corresponding amount.

YOU WILL NEED:
for coat:
$1\frac{1}{2}$ yds 48 in. wide fur material
$1\frac{1}{2}$ yds 36 in. wide lining material
$\frac{1}{3}$ yd of interfacing
Matching sewing thread
Buttonhole twist
Seam binding (optional)
Small button for neck
$3\frac{3}{4}$ in. buttons

for hat:
$\frac{1}{2}$ yd. 48 in. wide fur material
Matching sewing thread
Grosgrain ribbon
Elastic

1

Pin interfacing to W.S. of coat fronts. Attach curved edge of interfacing to coat body by herringbone stitch.

2

Pin, tack and stitch lining pockets to R.S. of coat fronts and coat back, matching notches.

3

R.S. back and fronts together, pin, tack and stitch shoulder seams.

4

R.S. together, pin, tack and stitch side seams, starting at underarm, continuing around pocket and down to hem.

5

R.S. together, stitch center seam of under collar. Stitch interfacing collar but overlap seam allowance at center back.

6

Place interfacing on to W.S. of under-collar. Tack around edge. Stitch rows $\frac{1}{2}$ in. apart, top to bottom, right across collar.

7

Pin R.S. of lining under-collar to R.S. of coat fabric at neck edge. Tack and stitch between dots.

Each square = 3 inches

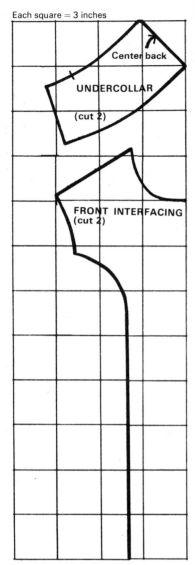

Center back

UNDERCOLLAR

(cut 2)

FRONT INTERFACING
(cut 2)

PATTERN FOR INTERFACING

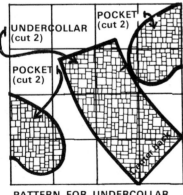

POCKET
(cut 2)

UNDERCOLLAR
(cut 2)

POCKET
(cut 2)

Center back

PATTERN FOR UNDERCOLLAR

AND POCKETS IN LINING

Each square = 3 inches

TOP SLEEVE AND
TOP SLEEVE LINING

(sleeve head)

BACK FACING

(front of sleeve)

FRONT FACING
(cut in fur fabric only)

UNDER SLEEVE AND
UNDER SLEEVE LINING

SELVEDGES

button and buttonhole positions

(pocket position)

(pocket position)

FRONT COAT AND
FRONT COAT LINING

BACK COAT AND BACK COAT LINING. FOLD

TOP COLLAR
(cut in fur fabric only)

PATTERN FOR COAT

NB shaded area=pattern pieces to be cut in lining
material also.

42

R.S. together, pin, tack and stitch back neck facing to front neck facings.

R.S. together, pin upper collar to facing. Tack and stitch between dots. (At this stage, coat is quite separate from facings and upper collar.)

R.S. together, pin upper collar and facing to coat and under-collar. Tack, easing upper collar to fit. Stitch.

R.S. together, pin, tack and stitch undersleeves to top sleeves, along both seams.

R.S. together, match notches and tack sleeves into position, adjusting ease. Stitch.

Turn up 1½ in. hem on sleeve bottoms. Slip stitch into position.

Using running stitch, sew a gathering thread, along upper sleeve head.

Turn up hem of coat to fit child. Use seam binding on hem if you prefer. (See 'hems' page 10.) Pin in position, tack and slip stitch into position.

Cut out lining and make up—R.S. together, stitch shoulder seams and then continue as for coat on side seams and sleeves.

Turn up hem of lining so that it is 1 in. above the hem of the coat. Tack and slip stitch this hem.

R.S. coat facing and lining together, stitch lining to facing starting at the hem and continuing around the neck to the other hem.

Turn to right side out. Slip stitch undersleeve of coat to undersleeve of lining at armhole seam, so lining does not slip around.

Slip stitch shoulder seams of coat to coat lining, to hold in position and prevent lining from slipping.

Turn back front facings of coat and slip stitch into position at hem.

Turn sleeve lining hem to W.S. and slip stitch to coat sleeve. Allow some ease so sleeve hangs correctly.

Make hand buttonholes using buttonhole twist. (On right front for a girl and left front for a boy.)

Sew buttons in place. Work a loop at top of facing same side as buttonholes. Sew on button on opposite side.

HAT: R.S. together, pin, tack and stitch sections together to make crown. Make lining in same way.

W.S. together, place lining inside cap. Tack around raw edges to hold lining and cap together.

Run a gathering thread along 2 panels. (This will be the peak.)

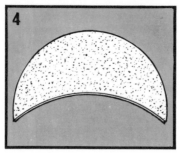

Place interfacing on W.S. of one peak shape.

Place R.S. of peak pieces together and stitch through the two pieces of peak and one layer of interfacing.

Turn peak to R.S. Pin to R.S. of crown along gathering thread. A seam of crown should be in center of peak. Tack.

Pin elastic to remainder of crown edge. Stretch elastic as you pin. Stitch both sides of elastic.

Stitch grosgrain to peak, finishing $\frac{3}{4}$ in. either side of peak and overlapping elastic. Hand sew corners of grosgrain to inside.

By hand, sew the center back of the elastic to the inside of the crown.

The hat pattern is for a head approximate size 21 in. For a smaller size, when making the pattern, reduce the width of each of the eight sections by the desired amount, and use a correspondingly smaller amount of elastic. For a larger size increase both width of crown sections and length of elastic.

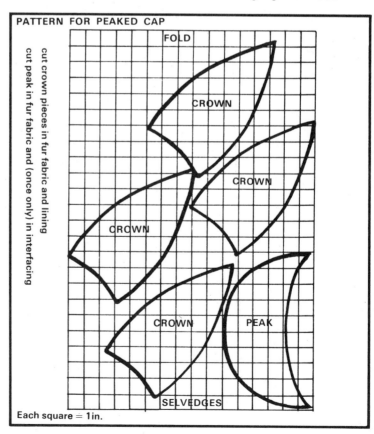

PATTERN FOR PEAKED CAP

FOLD

cut crown pieces in fur fabric and lining
cut peak in fur fabric and (once only) in interfacing

CROWN

CROWN

CROWN

CROWN

PEAK

SELVEDGES

Each square = 1 in.

Zip-fronted Shirt

This little shirt will suit boys and girls alike. Remember to take extra care when putting in the zipper as it is the main feature of the garment.

YOU WILL NEED:
1½ yds 36 in. wide
  lightweight jersey
Matching sewing thread
Matching zipper

TO ADJUST YOUR PATTERN:

The pattern is in Size 6.

For a size larger make the following adjustments:

FRONT: Widen pattern at side seam by $\frac{1}{4}$ in.
                Widen pattern at armhole level by $\frac{1}{4}$ in.
                Adjust neck to fit your child.
                Lengthen shirt by 1 in.

BACK: As for front.

SLEEVE: Widen sleeves by $\frac{1}{4}$ in. at either side at underarm seam.
                Lengthen sleeves by 1 in.

For a size smaller make the same adjustments but as reductions.

PATTERN FOR ZIP-FRONT SHIRT

Each square = 3 inches

1 Carefully insert zipper at center front. R.S. together, pin, tack and stitch shoulder seams. Topstitch seams on R.S. garment.

2 R.S. together, stitch collar to undercollar. Turn to right side. Press and topstitch.

3 R.S. together, tack collar to shirt. Cut crossway strip 1 in. wide, same length as collar. Stitch edge to collar edge.

4 Turn opposite edge over and slipstitch to cover raw edges of collar and top of shirt. With R.S. together, stitch in sleeves.

5 Topstitch around armhole seams on R.S. garment. Then W.S. together, stitch side seams and underarm seams.

6 Turn up 1 in. hem on sleeves and bottom of shirt. Topstitch two rows of stitching around each hem on R.S. garment.

Fur-Fronted Jacket and Cap

What little boy wouldn't be thrilled with this jacket and hat? Quick and easy to make, the fronts are imitation fur.

TO ADJUST YOUR PATTERN:
The jacket is in Size 6.
For a larger size make the following adjustments:
BACK: Increase neck length by $\frac{1}{8}$ in.
                  Increase shoulder seam by $\frac{1}{8}$ in.
                  Increase total length by $\frac{3}{4}$ in.
                  Deepen armhole by $\frac{1}{2}$ in.
FRONT: As for back.
SLEEVE: Widen sleeve by $\frac{1}{4}$ in. either side.
                  Lengthen sleeves by $\frac{3}{4}$ in.
For a smaller size decrease by a corresponding amount.
The hat fits a 21 in. head.

YOU WILL NEED:
for jacket:
1 yd 36 in. wide fabric
   (gabardine or similar)
$\frac{1}{2}$ yd 36 in. wide fur fabric
Matching Sewing Thread
Purchased Knitted Ribbing
Velcro

for hat:
$\frac{2}{3}$ yd 36 in. wide fabric
   (as jacket)
Purchased Knitted Fabric
Matching Sewing Thread
Buckles

FUR FRONTED JACKET: Place W.S. of fur fronts on R.S. jacket fronts. Fold fur to the back of the jacket, to find where side seam will be, as shown. Stitch along side seams (with R.S. fur to R.S. *back* of jacket) and fold fur back to jacket fronts.

Tack shoulder and front edges of fur to jacket to hold in place.

R.S. together, pin, tack and stitch shoulder seams, including fur fronts.

Cut a strip of knitted ribbing 16 in × 5 in. Fold in half and stitch raw edges to R.S. lower edge of jacket.

Place R.S. of front bands to R.S. of jacket fronts (on top of fur). Stitch in place.

Fold half of each band over to W.S. Turn under raw edges and slip stitch in place.

Sew Velcro to R.S. of right hand front band and W.S. of left hand front band, following maker's instructions.

PATTERN FOR BOYS FUR-FRONTED JACKET

Each square = 3 inches

SELVEDGES

(underarm seam)

SLEEVE

(front)

JACKET FRONT

(cut 2 fur fronts using jacket front pattern only)

(sleeve head)

(center underarm)

JACKET BACK

(underarm seam)

FRONT BANDS

(neck edge) →

FOLD

8

Cut a strip of knitted ribbing 12½ in. x 3 in. Place one raw edge to R.S. of neck edge. Pin, tack and stitch in place.

9

Turn over to W.S. so approximately 1 in. shows on R.S. Turn under to cover raw edges, and slip stitch in place.

10

R.S. inside, pin, tack and stitch along sleeve seams.

11

Cut 2 strips of knitted ribbing 5 in. × 5 in. Fold in half and stitch down long edge. Fold over. Stitch to R.S. sleeves at cuff.

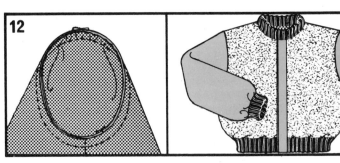

12

R.S. together, pin, tack and stitch sleeve into jacket.

CAP: R.S. together, tack and stitch side crown to top crown, matching dots. Make up crown lining in same way.

Place R.S. crown and lining together. Fold knitted fabric lengthways; insert between, all raw edges together. Stitch.

Turn hat right side out, so knitted fabric is on edge. R.S. together, tack and stitch crown to neckband.

R.S. together, place neckband lining on neckband. Tack and stitch around edges (except at base of crown). Trim turning and turn lining to W.S. Turn in neck edge and slip stitch lining to base of crown.

Fold straps lengthwise, W.S. inside and stitch along both edges. Fold in raw edges at end and stitch. Sew on buckles.

Sew straps and buckles to hat.

PATTERN FOR HAT

Each square = 3 inches

FOLD

NECKBAND (cut in fabric and lining)

SIDE CROWN LINING

TOP CROWN AND TOP CROWN LINING

SIDE CROWN (match dots with top crown)

STRAPS

SELVEDGES

Cape for Rainy Days

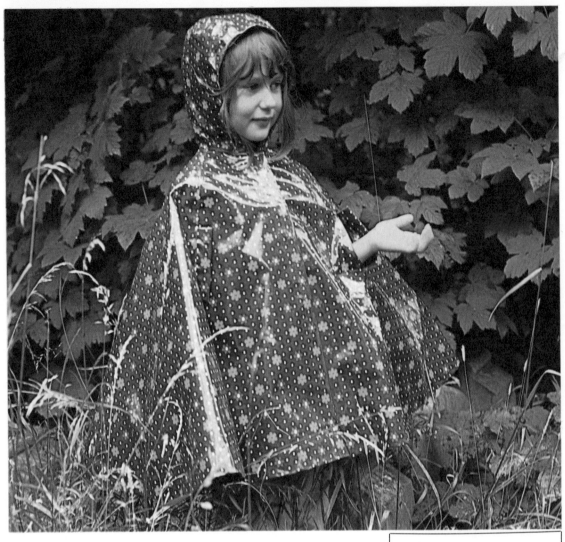

Colorful vinyl helps to brighten up those cloudy skies, and boys and girls alike will keep dry beneath this lovely cape and hood.

TO ADJUST YOUR PATTERN:
The pattern is in Size 5.
For a size larger make the following adjustments:
BACK CAPE: Increase neck length by $\frac{1}{16}$ in.
                      Increase cape length by 2 in.
FRONT CAPE: As for back.
HOOD: Increase hood center width by $\frac{1}{8}$ in. either side.
For cape size 4 decrease by corresponding amount.

YOU WILL NEED:
$2\frac{1}{2}$ yds 36 in. wide fabric
   (vinyl or similar)
$\frac{1}{2}$ yd 36 in. wide lining fabric
Matching Sewing Thread
Velcro
Glue

R.S. together, fold pocket flap in half and stitch along short sides. Turn to right side out.

R.S. together, stitch pocket flaps to back of cape.

R.S. together, stitch cape fronts to cape backs, leaving pocket flap free.

Glue seams down on wrong side to keep them flat. (Follow maker's instructions on adhesive carefully.)

R.S. together, stitch center back seam. Glue seam turnings down.

Turn up hem to fit child around bottom of raincoat and glue in place.

Fold fronts of cape to inside along fold lines marked. (Note this is not the center front line.)

Fold $\frac{1}{2}$ in. at top of facing to inside. Clip edge so it lies flat and glue in position.

PATTERN FOR RAINCAPE   FOLD

(side seam)

(neck edge)

POSITION FOR POCKET FLAP

POCKET FLAP

BACK CAPE

(back Center seam)

SELVEDGES

(neck edge)

FRONT CAPE

(side seam)

(neck edge)

(Center front line)

(fold line)

HOOD SIDES

HOOD CENTER

(cut one only)

(match notches with those on Hood Center)

(front edge)

Each square = 3 inches

9

Stitch Velcro $\frac{1}{2}$ in. from edge on R.S. of left front of cape. Stitch $\frac{1}{2}$ in. in from edge of W.S. of right front.

10

R.S. together, stitch hood sides to hood center, easing around curves.

11

Glue seams to keep them flat as you did on cape seams.

12

Make up hood lining in the same way, but do not glue seams. R.S. together, stitch lining to hood around front seam.

13

Turn lining to inside. With R.S. of hood to R.S. of cape, stitch together around neck.

14

Turn under raw edges of lining and slip stitch onto neck seam.

Night-time for Little Girls

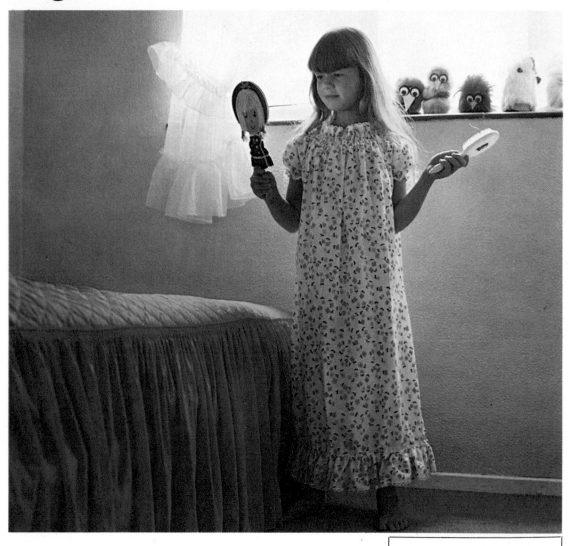

Refreshingly cool and pretty, any little girl will love this dreamy nightie. Our instructions tell you how to make a pair of baby doll pajamas too using the same pattern.

TO ADJUST YOUR PATTERN:
The pattern is in Size 6.
To make the pattern a size larger adjust as follows:
FRONT: Lengthen nightdress by 3 in.
             Widen by $\frac{1}{2}$ in.
BACK: As front.
SLEEVES: Lengthen sleeves by 1 in.
             Widen sleeves by $\frac{1}{2}$ in.
To make a size smaller make the same adjustments but as reductions.
However, for one smaller size use the sleeve pattern of a size 6.

YOU WILL NEED:
$2\frac{1}{8}$ yds 36 in. wide fabric
   (Make sure it is
   fire retardant).
Matching Sewing Thread
Shirring elastic
Lace

NIGHTDRESS: R.S. of frill together, stitch the seams. Turn under a small hem and tack and lace in position as close to the edge as possible. Stitch in place.

Run a gathering thread round the other edge of the frill.

R.S. together, pin, tack and stitch side seams of nightdress.

Pull up gathers of frill and adjust so it fits evenly around bottom of nighdress. R.S. together, pin, tack and stitch in place.

R.S. inside, stitch underarm seam of sleeves.

R.S. together, stitch sleeves to nighdress.

Turn under a small hem on bottom of sleeves and right around neck. Pin and tack lace close to the edge and stitch in position.

Put shirring elastic on the bobbin of your machine (follow maker's instructions). Sew five rows of shirring around the neck of the nightdress $\frac{1}{4}$ in. apart. The first line should be $\frac{3}{4}$ in. from the edge.

Stitch 2 rows of shirring elastic around sleeve hem $\frac{1}{2}$ in. from the edge.

PATTERN FOR NIGHTDRESS AND BABYDOLL PAJAMAS

Each square = 3 inches

FOLD

(sleeve head)

SLEEVE

(match notches with front and back pieces)

(match notches with front and back pieces)

HEM FRILL

HEM FRILL

FRONT AND BACK

SELVEDGES

Cutting line for pajama top

Each square = 3 inches

FOLD

SELVEDGES

Pajama Pants
BACK

Pajama Pants
FRONT

Pajama Pants
GUSSET

1

PAJAMAS: Follow the pattern for the nightdress, but cut out tops on the dotted line. Then make up in exactly the same way as the nightdress.

2

Pants: R.S. together, pin, tack and stitch side seams.

3

R.S. together, pin, tack and stitch gusset to pants.

4

Turn small hem to W.S. around legs. Pin, tack and stitch lace in position.

5

Stitch 2 rows of shirring elastic around legs, $\frac{1}{2}$ in. from edge.

6

Fold $1\frac{1}{2}$ in. at top of pants to wrong side and hem down leaving a small opening.

7

Cut elastic to fit child's waist. Thread around top of pants and stitch ends together. Slip stitch opening.

Judo Pajamas and Bathrobe

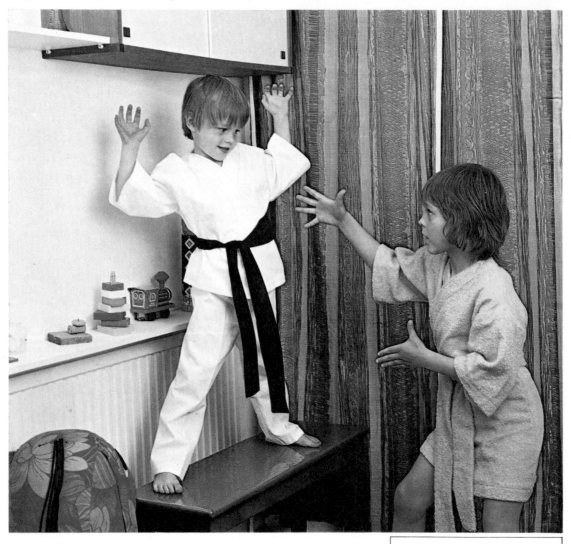

These judo pajamas will be such a favorite, they will doubtless make bedtime much easier! The pattern for the top can be used to make a terrific bathrobe.

TO ADJUST YOUR PATTERN:
The pattern is in Size 6.
For a size larger make the following adjustments:
Jacket:
FRONT: Widen side seams by $\frac{1}{4}$ in.
           Widen at shoulder seams by $\frac{1}{4}$ in.
           Lengthen by $1\frac{1}{4}$ in.
BACK: As for front.
SLEEVE: Widen each side by $\frac{1}{4}$ in.
           Lengthen by $1\frac{1}{4}$ in.
Pants:
           Widen pants at crotch level by $\frac{1}{4}$ in. each side.
           Extend waist upwards by 1 in.
           Lengthen by $1\frac{1}{2}$ in.
For a smaller size make the same adjustments but as reductions.

YOU WILL NEED:
for pajamas
3 yds 36 in. wide fabric
$\frac{1}{2}$ yd 36 in. wide fabric for belt
Matching Sewing Thread
2 Buttons
Waist Elastic

for bathrobe
2 yds 36 in. wide fabric (preferably toweling)
Matching Sewing Thread

JUDO PAJAMAS AND BATHROBE: R.S. together, pin, tack and stitch shoulder seams on the jacket and facing.

Stitch R.S. of facing to W.S. of fronts and neck of jacket.

Turn facing to the front of garment. Turn under raw edges, pin, tack and topstitch 2 rows as shown.

R.S. together, pin, tack and stitch side seams.

R.S. together pin, tack and stitch underarm sleeve seams.

R.S. together, stitch sleeves into jacket.

Turn under a $1\frac{1}{2}$ in. hem around bottom of jacket and sleeves. Stitch in place. Cut belt material in 7 in. wide strips and join to make a belt 54 in. long.

Fold in half lengthways; stitch around, leaving a small opening. Pull belt through to R.S. and slip stitch opening.

To make pants: R.S. together, pin, tack and stitch back seam of pants.

Turn a $\frac{1}{2}$ in. hem to wrong side of pants top and tack in place.

PATTERN FOR JUDO PAJAMAS

Each square = 3 inches

FLY FRONT (cut one only)

(elastic stops here)

PANTS

(front)

(back)

FRONT FACING

FRONT

(inside leg seam)

(inside leg seam)

SELVEDGES

BACK NECK FACING

BACK (cut one only)

(sleeve head)

(front)

SLEEVES

FOLD

11

Measure child's waist, and cut elastic to fit comfortably. Lay elastic along top of pants and stitch it $\frac{3}{8}$ in. from the top edge stretching it as you go. Stitch 3 more parallel rows, approximately $\frac{3}{8}$ in. apart.

12

R.S. together, pin, tack and stitch fly front to left hand side of pajama front.

13

Turn facing to back of garment. Turn under to cover raw edges and tack. Machine stitch a line of stitching along turning.

14

Turn under fly piece on right hand side of pajamas. Turn to cover raw edge, tack and stitch 1 row along turning.

15

R.S. together, pin, tack and stitch along crotch seam, overlapping left to right facing.

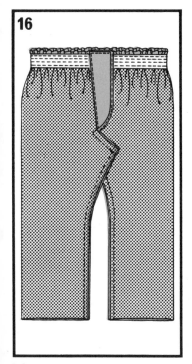

16

R.S. together, pin, tack and stitch along inside leg seam.

17

Turn under $1\frac{1}{2}$ in. hem on legs and stitch. Make two buttonholes on top right hand side and sew buttons on left front facing.

18

BATHROBE: Extend jacket pattern to desired length and make in exactly the same way using a toweling material.

Sunny Day Clothes

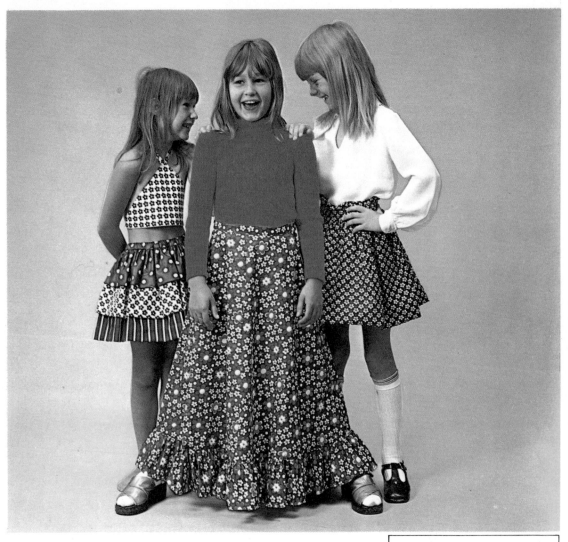

Skirts and a sun dress for cool wear on sunny days. Best of all — they are quick and simple to make. The sun dress is made from strips of material — no need even for a pattern! Instructions for sun dress are on the opposite page.)

TO ADJUST YOUR PATTERN:
The Sundress is Size 5.
For a larger size increase the size of the square by $\frac{1}{2}$ in. all around. Increase the skirts to required length. For smaller sizes decrease accordingly.

Skirts:
The pattern is Size 8.
For smaller or larger sizes, adjust pieces to child's waist size and height.

YOU WILL NEED:
for the sundress:
1 yd 36 in. wide fabric
$\frac{1}{2}$ yd 36 in. wide fabric — contrasting print
$\frac{3}{4}$ yd 36 in. wide fabric — contrasting print
Matching Sewing Thread
$\frac{1}{2}$ in. wide elastic for waist

for the long skirt:
$2\frac{1}{2}$ yd 36 in. wide fabric
Matching Sewing Thread
6 in. zipper. Snaps

for the short skirt:
1 yd 36 in. wide fabric
Matching Sewing Thread
2 in. wide ribbed elastic.

SUN DRESS: From 1st print, cut a 12 in. square, 4 strips 1½ in. x 15 in. and 2 strips 10½ in. x 15 in. for bodice, ties and middle skirt. From 2nd print cut 2 strips 7 in. x 36 in. and 1 strip 3 in. x 28 in. for top skirt and waist band. From 3rd print cut 2 pieces 13½ in. x 36 in. for lower skirt.

W.S. inside, fold in one end of each tie. Fold in raw edges right along. Pin, tack and slip stitch sides together.

Turn ¾ in. turnings to W.S. all around the 12 in. square. Then fold square crosswise as shown.

Insert raw edges of ties at top point and sides. Pin, tack and stitch firmly in place. Stitch along open sides close to edge.

R.S. together, stitch along side seams of each of the 3 skirt lengths.

Turn under a 2 in. hem to the wrong side on each piece. Pin, tack and slip stitch in place.

W.S. inside, place top skirt over middle skirt and both skirts over lower one. Pin at top to hold together.

Run a gathering thread at top of all skirts and draw up to fit waistband.

Stitch side seam of waistband and then, with R.S. together, pin, tack and stitch waistband to top of all skirts.

Fold waistband over to wrong side of skirt. Turn over to cover raw edges and slip stitch, leaving a small opening.

Insert elastic to fit comfortably around child's waist. Stitch ends together. Slip stitch opening in waistband.

PATTERN FOR LONG SKIRT WITH FRILL

Each square = 3 inches

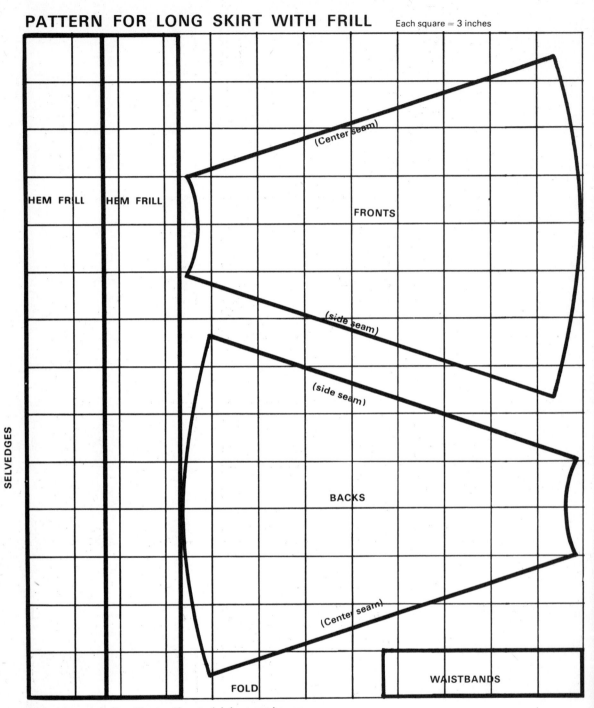

HEM FRILL   HEM FRILL

FRONTS

(Center seam)

(side seam)

(side seam)

BACKS

(Center seam)

SELVEDGES

FOLD

WAISTBANDS

N.B. pattern only fits this way if material does not have a one-way pattern.

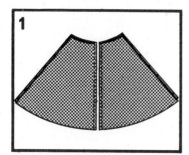

1

LONG SKIRT: R.S. together, pin, tack and stitch front skirts and back skirts down center seams.

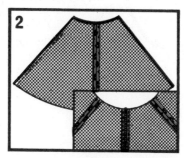

2

Pin, tack and stitch left hand side seam in the same way and insert zipper.

3

Pin, tack and stitch other side seam. R.S. together, pin, tack and stitch 1 edge of waistband around top of skirt.

4

Fold waistband over to wrong side, turn to cover raw edge and slip stitch in place. Slip stitch ends. Sew on snaps.

5

R.S. together, stitch side seams of hem frill together. Turn a small hem to W.S. on one edge and slip stitch in place.

6

Gather other side. R.S. together and adjusting gathers, pin, tack and stitch frill to lower edge of skirt.

1

SHORT SKIRT: From a square yard of material, cut 2 strips 18 in. x 32 in. The remaining strip (4 in. x 36 in.) is for the waistband.

2

R.S. of large strips together, stitch down shorter seams. Pin, tack and stitch waistband seam in the same way.

3

Run a gathering thread around top of skirt. R.S. together, pin, tack and stitch to the waistband.

4

Turn 1 in. of waistband to W.S. at top. Pin elastic $\frac{1}{2}$ in. from top edge (inside skirt).

5

Machine stitch elastic to waistband, stretching elastic as you stitch. Stitch 4 rows $\frac{1}{4}$ in. distances apart.

6

Turn a $2\frac{1}{2}$ in. hem to W.S. at bottom of skirt. Slip stitch in place.

Party Dress for Sophisticates

A dream dress — romantic and pretty, but just right for an 8-11 year old. Make it from light cotton for a floating effect.

TO ADJUST YOUR PATTERN:
The pattern is in Size 8.
For a larger size make the following adjustments:

FRONT BODICE: Widen chest by $\frac{1}{2}$ in.
Widen at center armhole level by $\frac{1}{4}$ in.
Lengthen shoulder by $\frac{1}{8}$ in.
Lengthen bodice by $\frac{1}{2}$ in.
Deepen armhole by $\frac{1}{4}$ in.

BACK BODICE: As for front.

FRONT SKIRT: Lengthen by $1\frac{1}{2}$ in.
Width remains the same.

BACK SKIRT: As front skirt.

SLEEVE: All sections of sleeve widen by $\frac{1}{2}$ in.
All sections of sleeve lengthen by $\frac{3}{8}$ in.

BOW, BELT & COLLAR: Remain the same.
For one size smaller make the adjustments as reductions.

YOU WILL NEED:
$4\frac{2}{3}$ yds 36 in. wide fabric
1 yd 36 in. wide contrasting plain fabric
Matching Sewing Thread
14 in. zipper.
$\frac{1}{4}$ in. wide elastic
Bias Binding

LONG PARTY DRESS: Cut 2 lengths of fabric 36 in. square for skirt pieces. Cut a small slit at center of one for zipper.

R.S. together, pin, tack and stitch skirt side seams.

R.S. together, stitch long edges and one short edge of belt pieces. Turn right side out and press.

Stitch darts shown on pattern in front and back bodices.

R.S. together, pin, tack and stitch shoulder and bodice side seams, with belt ties in place at waist edge.

Run a gathering thread around top of skirt. R.S. together, pin, tack and stitch skirt to bodice, adjusting gathers evenly.

W.S. inside, fold collar and turn in ends. Run gathering thread along raw edges. Draw up to fit neck.

Pin and tack collar to outside neck. Insert zipper in center back, extending slit in skirt if necessary.

Stitch shoulder seams of neck facing. R.S. together, pin, tack and stitch facing to collar and dress. Turn facing to W.S.

Join contrast color crossway strips to trim lower sleeves. Fold lengthways, press, stitch to R.S. top of lower sleeve.

R.S. together, stitch seam of lower sleeves (crossway strip folded to R.S.) Sew bias binding around cuff edge. Turn to inside.

Slip stitch in place leaving opening for elastic. Thread elastic through and sew ends securely. Slip stitch opening.

FOLD

LOWER SLEEVE

BELT TIES

(front)

(sleeve head)

TOP SLEEVE

MIDDLE SLEEVE

FRONT BOW PIECE

SELVEDGES

COLLAR (cut one only)

SKIRT CUT SEPARATELY

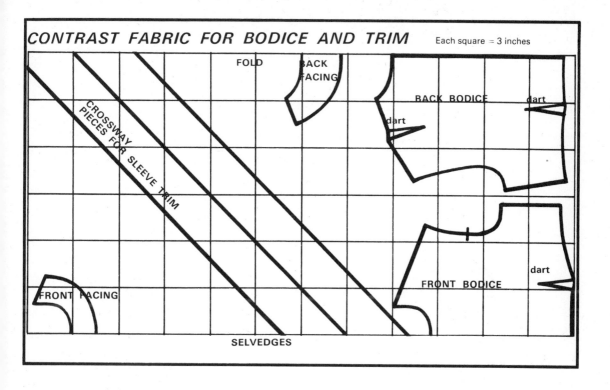

CONTRAST FABRIC FOR BODICE AND TRIM

Each square = 3 inches

FOLD

BACK FACING

BACK BODICE

dart

dart

CROSSWAY PIECES FOR SLEEVE TRIM

FRONT BODICE

dart

FRONT FACING

SELVEDGES

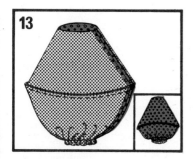

13

R.S. inside, stitch seam of middle sleeves. R.S. together, stitch middle to lower sleeves (strip stands out on R.S.).

14

Work smocking on upper sleeve as shown on page 13. R.S. inside, stitch top sleeve seam, then top sleeve to middle sleeve.

15

Run gathering thread around head of top sleeve. Draw up to fit armhole. Pin, tack and stitch to dress, adjusting gathers.

16

Fold bow piece R.S. inside, stitch along long edge and one short edge. Turn to right side and slip stitch end.

17

Tie into a bow and sew at center of bodice, just below collar. Turn up hem on skirt to fit. Slip stitch in place.

Smart Check Pants

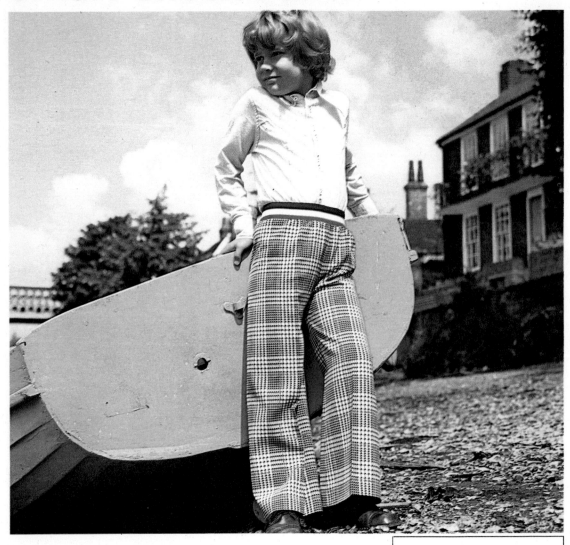

A terrific pair of pants that are ideal for girls and boys. The elasticized waist means no fussing to put in zips. Easy to make and great to wear.

TO ADJUST YOUR PATTERN:
The pattern is in Size 6.
For a size larger make the following adjustments.
Lengthen trouser by $1\frac{1}{2}$ in. crotch to hem.
Extend crotch to waist seam upwards by $\frac{1}{2}$ in.
Cut the pattern along the "side seam" level and open out by $\frac{3}{4}$ in.
Redraw outline of pattern.
For a size smaller make the same adjustments but as reductions.

YOU WILL NEED:
1yd 54in. wide fabric
Matching sewing thread
Elastic braid trim

PATTERN FOR PANTS

FOLD

(inside leg seam)

Center back

PANTS

(Top)

Center front

(inside leg seam)

SELVEDGES

(NB PANTS are cut in 2 pieces – there are no side seams)   Each square = 3 inches

R.S. together, pin, tack and stitch leg seams.

R.S. together, pin, tack and stitch crotch seams.

Cut elastic braid trim to required length for waist fitting. Overlap ends and stitch together.

Divide waistband into four. R.S. together, pin each point at center front and back and left and right sides. Tack and stitch at top and bottom of elastic stretching it as you sew.

Turn up hems around bottom of legs to fit child and slip stitch in place.

73

Knitting and Crochet

Garments in this section of the book have all been made by hand knitting, and some of them are finished off with crochet stitches. On this and the next few pages we give implicit instructions for how to knit and crochet as well as some general points of pressing and sewing up of garments and checking knitting tension. If you already know how to knit and crochet, we would still advise you to read the general notes which ensure the very best results for knitted garments. In all our patterns figures in brackets refer to the larger sizes respectively. Where only one figure is given, it refers to all sizes.

CASTING ON

Begin by leaving a length of yarn according to the number of stitches to be cast on, then make a slip knot, and put this onto the Needle.

Loop the long thread of yarn hanging from the knot over your left thumb. Hold the needle in your right hand with the yarn coming from ball of wool at the back. Loop this over your right hand index and third finger as shown in the illustration. Insert the point of the needle into the loop, wrap the wool in your right hand once around the needle and draw a loop through, so you now have two loops on the needle. Pull the thread quite tight. Repeat for the number of stitches required.

HOW TO DO PLAIN OR KNIT STITCH

Cast on required number of stitches. Hold the needle with the cast on stitches in the left hand, with the point approximately $\frac{1}{2}$ in. above the thumb and first finger. With the other Needle in the right hand, insert the point from right to left through the first loop, pass the yarn, which in plain knitting is always at the back of the work, around the point of the right hand Needle and draw a loop through. Keep this loop on the right hand Needle, and let the old stitch slide off the left hand Needle.

Continue to the end of the row. For the next row, turn the knitting around and pass the empty Needle back into the right hand.

HOW TO DO PURL STITCH

Cast on. Hold the Needle with the cast on stitches in the left hand, as for Knit stitch, but keep the yarn always to the front of the work. Insert the right hand Needle from right to left through the first loop to the front instead of the back as in the Knit stitch. Now pass the yarn around the point of the Needle and draw a loop through. Keep this loop on the right hand Needle, and let the old stitch slide off the left hand Needle. Continue to the end of the row. Turn knitting around, and pass the empty needle into the right hand.

GARTER STITCH
This consists of 'Knit' rows throughout.

RIBBING
Ribbing consists of Knit and Purl stitches worked alternately in the same row, and produces a very elastic fabric for cuffs, welts, and neckbands, etc. The type of rib required for each pattern is always stated, e.g. K.2, P.2 rib means 2 Knit stitches, followed by 2 Purl stitches, all along the row.

HOW TO DECREASE
To decrease 1 stitch at the beginning of a row: Slip 1 stitch, K. 1 stitch, pass the slipped stitch over the Knitted stitch.
To decrease 1 stitch at the end of a row: Knit the last 2 stitches together.
For Purl, follow the same instructions, reading Purl instead of Knit.

HOW TO INCREASE
Knit or Purl into the stitch, and before slipping it off the Needle, Knit or Purl again into the back of the loop.

CASTING OFF
Generally, the cast off row in S.S. is a Knit row, but where it is a Purl row, read Purl for Knit in the following instructions: Knit the first 2 sts., * slip the first st. over the second, leaving 1 st. on the right hand Needle. Knit the next st., then repeat from * until 1 st. remains. Break the yarn, and draw the end right through the loop.
When working a pattern, always cast off in the pattern. This is particularly important for ribbing, or the edge may break in wear.

STOCKING STITCH (S.S.)
This consists of one Knit row and one Purl row worked alternately. The Knit side is generally considered the right side.

GENERAL POINTS

When it is necessary to begin a new ball of wool in knitting, it should always be joined at the end of the row. Leave a small length of the new ball of wool at the side and hold on to it as you knit the first few stitches of the row to ensure they are tightly knitted. When you have knitted back across this row, pull both ends of wool tightly again.

When knitting is finished, thread loose ends on to a darning needle and secure them by taking half a dozen or so small oversewing stitches along the outside of the work.

When all pieces are knitted, pin them out on an ironing board or table for pressing. Place the pins approximately $\frac{1}{2}$in. apart and pin the work to the correct measurement. It is not necessary to pin out the ribbing and ribbing areas should never be pressed as it flattens them.

To press the knitting, steam each piece carefully by using a hot iron over a damp cloth. Do not put pressure on to the knitting, thus allowing the steam to penetrate, and do not remove the pins until each piece has cooled. If you have knitted with synthetic yarns, press with a cool iron and a dry cloth only and always follow the yarn manufacturer's instructions for washing and pressing.

Sew each piece together with small back stitches and do not pull too tightly as you sew or the seams will be puckered. Press the seams carefully in the same way as you did the individual pieces.

Always knit a tension square before beginning a garment to be sure you can obtain the stated stitches and rows per inch. Instructions for this are given on page 77.

HOW TO CHECK TENSION

Using the yarn and size of Needles stated in the instructions, work a piece of fabric not less than 3 inches square in the appropriate stitch. Carefully measure the stitches and rows to the inch.

As the work of individual knitters varies in tightness, you may find that you cannot obtain the correct row tension, even though the stitches are correct. This does not matter in most cases, as most knitting instructions are based on measurement in inches rather than stating a certain number of rows to be worked. However, if a certain number of rows is specified, and you know that you did not obtain the correct row tension on your test piece, you must note the difference between the two tensions, and adjust the rows you knit accordingly, either by subtracting rows if you have fewer rows to the inch, or adding rows if you have more. For example, suppose the row tension stated is 8 rows to the inch, and the instructions state work 24 rows, then the work will measure 3 in. long. If, for instance, you have only 6 rows to the inch, and you work 24 rows, your work will measure 4 in. Therefore, you must subtract 1 in. (6 rows), in order to obtain the correct measurement. If, on the other hand, you have 10 rows to the inch, and you work 24 rows, your work will measure approximately $2\frac{1}{2}$ in. Therefore, you must add $\frac{1}{2}$ in. (5 rows), in order to obtain the correct measurement.

It is essential to obtain the correct number of stitches to the inch. A size smaller or larger Needle than that stated may be used to adjust this; smaller Needles will give you more stitches to the inch, and larger needles will give you fewer.

ABBREVIATIONS

The following abbreviations are used commonly in knitting patterns.

K	= Knit (plain stitch)		n.r.	= Next Row
P	= Purl		Sts	= Stitches
SS	= Stocking Stitch		inc	= Increase stitches
G.S.	= Garter Stitch		dec	= Decrease stitches
r	= Row		tog	= Together (as in K2 sts tog.)
			F.I.	= Fair Isle
			beg.	= Beginning

CROCHET

We have used crochet to trim some of our knitted garments, and specific instructions for working this are given below. First of all however, we give instructions for making a chain, which is the equivalent of casting on in knitting.

TO WORK A CHAIN

Fold yarn (close to the end) into a loop. Using the crochet hook pull yarn through to make a slip knot and leave this loop on the hook. Hold the crochet hook between the thumb and index finger of your right hand. Hold yarn or chain between thumb and second finger of your left hand and loop the wool over the index finger of your left hand. You can then use the crochet hook to twist around the wool. (Reverse all instructions if you are left handed).

Holding the yarn and hook as described, with one loop on

the hook twist yarn around hook once. Hold base of slip
knot with left hand as described and pull hook with yarn
through the loop on the hook to make a new one. Repeat
this procedure until work is required length. (The illustration
on the right shows a close-up of the first stitch being
worked in a chain.)   •

TO MAKE A DOUBLE CROCHET EDGING

Hold the knitting horizontally with the right side facing you.
Crochet will be worked from right to left, one whole knitted
st. away from the edge. (Left-handed people work from left
to right). Knot the crochet yarn to the appropriate edge of
knitting, one whole st. away from the edge (i.e. under the
two top threads), and pick up crochet yarn. You should now
have 1 loop on hook.

2. Insert hook from the front under the two top strands of
the first knitted st. Catch yarn with hook. (This is known as
"thread over".) Draw yarn through knitted fabric. (2 loops on
hook).

3. Thread over hook and draw through 2 loops on hook – 1
loop remains on hook. This completes 1 double crochet st.

4. To make next double crochet st. insert hook from the
front under the two top strands of the next knitted st.
Thread over hook. Now continue working along the knitted
edge, repeating steps 3 to 5 throughout.

GENERAL POINTS

It is not always necessary to work 1 double crochet st. into every knitted st. This depends on the thickness of the knitting yarn, but the important thing is always to keep the work flat, so space the crochet sts. accordingly, and if it is necessary to miss spaces, miss them evenly along the crochet r. If you work too many crochet sts., the knitting will stretch, and if you work too few, it will gather.

When you are working around a back opening, or along 2 front edges, they must match together. When you come to the second edge, pin it to the first edge as you work, to ensure a good match.

If 2 rs. of double crochet are specified in the instructions, when you reach the end of the first r., work 1 chain st. (simply thread over hook and draw through loop already on hook). Turn the work, so that the reverse faces you, and begin another r. of double crochet sts., working into the spaces formed by the first r.

Where button loops are required, work these in chain st. (the number of chains depending on the size of the buttons). Work the button loops at even intervals during the second r. of double crochet, missing the appropriate number of double crochet spaces in the first r. before re-starting double crochet. Remember that loops of wool tend to stretch, so do not make them too large, or the garment will gape in wear.

When joining 2 knitted pieces together with double crochet, hold the pieces with wrong sides together, and work crochet through both layers at once.

Baby's Hooded Cape

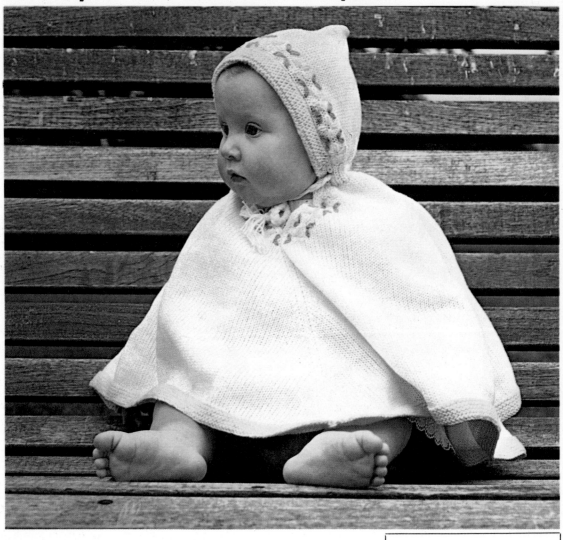

Just the thing to keep baby snug and warm on blowy days. This all-in-one cape and hood fits a baby approximately 6 months old.

TENSION:
7 sts. and 9 rs. to 1 inch, knitting S.S. on no. 10 ns.

YOU WILL NEED:
4 50 grm balls
    fingering yarn in main
    color (white)
1 50 grm ball in contrast
    color (pink)
Remnant of Green for embroidery
No. 3 and No. 1 Knitting
    needles
Size B crochet hook
4 stitch holders.

1

Using contrast color, and No. 3 ns, cast on 136 sts. Work 2 rs. G.S. *nr:* * K.2 k.2 tog., K to last 4 sts. K.2 tog, K.2. *nr:* K * Repeat from * to * 3 times. (See page 77 for abbreviations.)

2

Change to main color, and work in S.S. beg. with a K.r. K.2 K.2 tog., K to last 4 sts. K.2 tog., K.2 *nr:* P.

3

Repeat last 2 rs until 24 sts remain, ending with a P.r.

4

Shape neck – K.2, K.2 tog., K.4. Slip next 8 sts onto holder. Slip remaining 8 sts onto spare N.

5

nr: Cast off 2 sts at inner edge. P. to end. *nr:* K.2, K.2 tog. K to end. *nr:* as first row. *nr:* K.1, K.2 tog. Cast off.

6

Rejoin wool to inner end of sts on spare N. with R.S. facing *nr:* Cast off 2 sts, K. to end. *nr:* P.2, P.2 together, P to end. *nr:* as first r. *nr:* P.1 P.2 tog. Cast off remaining 2 sts.

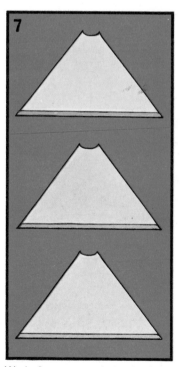

7

Work 3 more panels in the same way.

81

PATTERN FOR CAPE AND HOOD

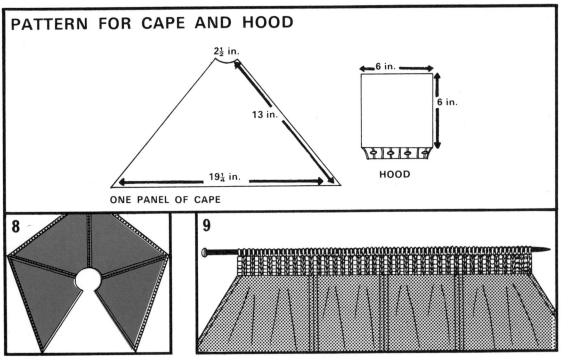

2½ in.

13 in.

19¼ in.

ONE PANEL OF CAPE

6 in.

6 in.

HOOD

8 Neckband – Join 3 side seams leaving 4th seam open.

9 Using No. 1 ns and main color, with W.S. of work facing, pick up 72 sts (including sts from holder). Work 4 rs K.1 P.1 rib.

10 *nr:* in K.1 P.1 rib, K.2 cast off next 2 sts., K.7*, repeat from * to * until 5 sts remain. Cast off next 2 sts. K.3 (8 holes). *nr:* in rib, K.3* cast on 2 sts. K.7* Repeat from * to * until 4 sts remain. Cast on 2 sts. K.2 Work 2 rs in rib.

11 *Hood* – Change to No. 3 Ns and in S.S. K.2*. Inc. into next st., K.5*. Repeat from * to * 10 more times. Inc. into next st. K.3 (84 sts). Work 55 rs in S.S. Cast off.

12 Fold hood in half and join top seam.

Hood Edging: In contrast color and No. 3 ns., right side facing, pick up 72 sts along front edge of hood between upper edges of ribbed neckband. Work 10 rs G.S. Cast off.

Fold back G.S. rs. along edge of hood and catch down. Join front seam of cape to within 4 in. of base of neckband.

With B crochet hook and main color, work 1r double crochet around neck opening.

Embroider lazy daisy st. flowers around hood and front opening.

Neck cord — cut 15 strands of main color yarn, about 1 yd long, and braid together in 3 groups of 5 strands.

Knot ends and trim tassels. Thread cord through neckband holes and tie.

Press finished garment gently with a warm iron over a dry cloth.

Knitted Popover Dress

This delightful little popover dress is very easy to make and enchanting to look at.

MEASUREMENTS:
Our pattern fits a child of 9 months (1 year, 18 months) — chest sizes 19 (19½, 20) inches. Figures in brackets refer to larger sizes respectively.

YOU WILL NEED:
3(3, 4) 50 grm balls of sport
     weight wool in main color
     (Turquoise)
1 50 grm ball sport weight wool
     in each of 3 contrasting colors
     (Royal Blue, White and Yellow)
No. 5, No. 3 and No. 1 Knitting
     Needles
Size B crochet hook
Stitch holder
3 small buttons
Flower motif

BACK — Using No. 5 Ns. cast on 118(120, 124) sts. Begin with a K.r. and work 6 rs in S.S. Change to No. 3 Ns. and continue until work measures 8(8½, 9) in. from cast-on edge, ending with a P.r.

Back opening — K. 59(60, 62) sts. Put remaining sts on holder. Turn, knit 2 in. ending with a K.r. — [59(60, 62)sts.]

** P.2 tog., *P.2 tog., P.1* Repeat from * to * until 0(1, 3) sts remain on needle. P. to end 39(40, 42) sts. *Bodice* — work S.S. in 2r stripes using 3 colors and main color. K.6rs. (You will need to work 1r extra here on other side of bodice.)

Shape armhole —*cast off 2 sts at beg. of next r. P.1 r.* Repeat from * to * 4(4,5) more times. Dec 1st at beg. of next r.

1st and 2nd sizes only — P. 1r Dec. 1 st at beg of next row. All sizes — 27(28, 29) sts. remain.

Shape neck — still in stripes, cast off 7(8, 9) sts at beg. of next r. K. 1r. *Cast off 2 sts at beg. of next r. K.1r* Repeat from * to * 4 more times (10 sts remain). Work 4¼(4¾, 5¼) in. from beg of armhole shaping ending with a P.r.

Shape shoulder — cast off 5 sts at beg of next r. Cast off remaining 5 sts.**

Pick up 59(60, 62) sts from holder. With R.S. facing rejoin wool to inner end of stitches. Work 2in. ending with a K.r. Follow instructions from ** to ** noting extra r. to be worked before armhole shaping.

Front — using main color and No. 5 Ns. cast on 118(120, 124) sts. Starting with K.r., work 6 rs. S.S. Change to No. 3 Ns. and continue until work measures 10(10½, 11) in. from cast-on edge, ending with a K.r.

1st size only — *P.1. P.2 tog. * Repeat from * to * until 4 sts remain. P.2 together twice (78sts). *2nd size* —* P.1. P.2 tog. * Repeat from * to * to end (80sts). *3rd size* – P.2,* P.1, P.2 tog.* Repeat from * to * until 2sts remain. P.2 (84sts.).

Bodice (stripes as back) K. 6rs. *Shape armholes* — cast off 2sts. at beg of next 10(10, 12) rs. Dec 1 at beg of next 4(4, 2) rs.

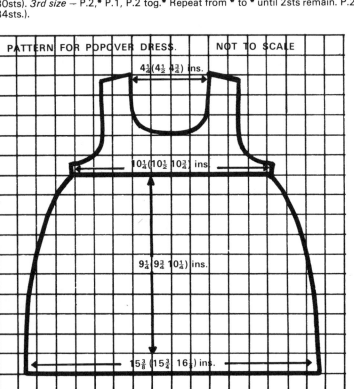

PATTERN FOR POPOVER DRESS. NOT TO SCALE

4¼(4½ 4¾) ins.

10½(10½ 10¾) ins

9¼(9¾ 10¼) ins.

15⅜(15¾ 16¼) ins.

To FIT a 19(19½ 20) in. chest

Diagram shows shape of dress. It is not drawn to scale.

K. 20sts., put 14(16, 18) sts. on to holder. Put 20sts on to spare N. Turn. * cast off 2sts. K.1r.* Repeat from * to * 4 more times (10sts.).

Continue until work is 4¼(4¾, 5¼) in. from armhole shaping (end with P.r.) Cast off 5 sts at beg of nr. K. to end. Cast off.

14

Pick up 20 sts from spare N. Rejoin wool at outer end of W.S. P.1r. Cast off 2sts at beg. of next r. P.1r.

15

Repeat from * to * 4 more times (10 sts remain). Continue until work measures $4\frac{1}{4}(4\frac{3}{4}, 5\frac{1}{4})$ in. from armhole shaping, ending with a K.r. Cast off 5 sts at beg. of next r. P. to end. Cast off remaining 5 sts.

16

Neckband — pin out each piece to size and press (see page 76). Take care not to press gathers flat. Join shoulder seams. Press. Using No. 1 Ns and main color. R.S. facing, pick up 118(122, 126) sts around neckline (including sts. from holder).

17

Work 6 rs of K.2. P.2 rib. Cast off in rib.

18

Armhole bands — (both alike). Using No. 1 Ns and main color, R.S. facing, pick up 52(56, 60) sts around armhole. Work 6 rs of K.2, P.2, rib. Cast off in rib.

19

Join side seams. Press. Fold 6 rs around lower edge to W.S. and catch down using cotton thread. Press carefully.

20

Using main color wool and size B crochet hook, work 2 rs double crochet around back opening. Include 3 chain st. button loops within striped section on right side edge in second row (see page 79). Sew on 3 buttons to correspond.

21

Sew motif into position and give a final light press.

Fair Isle for All

Fair Isle knitting looks so impressive, and it really is not so difficult to do. Follow our instructions to make these terrific garments — a trendy little tank top and a zip-up cardigan. Suitable for boys or girls, they are bound to be winners with all youngsters. (If Fair Isle knitting still seems a little too ambitious, follow the instructions for making the tank top in just one color.)

MEASUREMENTS (for tank top):
To fit a child of approximately 5(6, 7) years — chest sizes 23(24, 25) inches. For garment measurements, see diagram.

TENSION (for tank top):
$7\frac{1}{2}$ sts. 9 rs. 1 inch, knitting S.S. on No. 3 Needles.

YOU WILL NEED
(for tank top):
2(2, 3) 50grm. balls sportweight
  wool in main color
  (Yellow)
1 50grm. ball 4 ply wool
  in contrast color (Green)
A pair each of No. 1, No. 3
  and No. 4 Knitting Needles.
N.B. For a plain top, omit
  contrast wool and No. 4
  Knitting Needles.

BACK TO FRONT (both alike):
Using YELLOW wool and No. 1 Ns., cast on 86(90, 94) sts. Work 1½ inches of K.2, P.2 rib, increasing 6(5, 5) sts. evenly across the work in the last r. (92(95, 99) sts. altogether). Change to No. 3 Ns. and S.S., and starting with a K. r., work 4 rs. Change to No. 4 Ns. and using YELLOW (Y) and GREEN (G), work 29 rs. of Fair Isle as follows:

FAIR ISLE TOP ONLY:
(for plain top continue in S.S. for 29 rs. in ONE color only)
1st r: K.2(3,5)Y, *3G, 1Y. Repeat from * until 2(4,6) sts. remain. K. Y to end.
2nd r: P.4(6,8)Y, *1G, 3Y. Repeat from * until 0(1,2) sts. remain. P.Y to end.
3rd r: K.5(6,8)Y, *1G, 3Y. Repeat from * until 3(5,7) sts. remain. K.Y to end.
4th r: P.1(3,5)Y, 1G, 3Y. *3G, 1Y. Repeat from * until 3(4,6) sts. remain. P.1Y, 1G. P.Y to end.
5th r: K.1(2,4)Y, 2G. K.Y until 3(5,7) sts. remain. K.2G. K.Y to end.
6th r: P.1(3,5)Y, 1G, 2Y, 1G. P.Y until 5(6,8) sts. remain. P. 1G, 2Y, 1G. P.Y to end.
7th r: K.3(4,6)Y, 2G, 1Y, 2G, 3Y, 1G, 3Y, 1G, 23Y, 2G, 3Y, 1G, 3Y, 1G, 23Y, 2G, 3Y, 1G, 3Y, 1G, 5Y, 2G, K. Y to end.
8th r: P.1(3,5)Y, 1G, 2Y, 1G, 6Y, 1G, 2Y, 2G, 3Y, 1G, 9Y, 1G, 14Y, 1G, 2Y, 2G, 3Y, 1G, 9Y, 1G, 14Y, 1G, 2Y, 2G, 3Y, 1G, 1Y, 1G, 2Y, 1G, P, Y to end.
9th r: K1(2,4)Y, 2G, 3Y, 1G, 2Y, 1G, 1Y, 1G, 2Y, 1G, 13Y, 3G, 8Y, 1G, 2Y, 1G, 1Y, 1G, 2Y, 1G, 13Y, 3G, 8Y, 1G, 2Y, 1G, 1Y, 1G, 2Y, 1G, 8Y, 2G, K.Y to end.
10th r: P.1(3,5)Y, 1G, 2Y, 1G, 6Y, 1G, 1Y, 1G, 3Y, 3G, 4Y, 2G, 2Y, 3G, 2Y, 2G, 9Y, 1G, 1Y, 1G, 3Y, 3G, 4Y, 2G, 2Y, 3G, 2Y, 2G, 9Y, 1G, 1Y, 1G, 3Y, 3G, 1Y, 1G, 2Y, 1G, P. Y to end.

11th r: K.3(4,6)Y, 2G, 2Y, 2G, 4Y, 2G, 9Y, 2G, 3Y, 1G, 3Y, 2G, 5Y, 2G, 4Y, 2G, 9Y, 2G, 3Y, 1G, 3Y, 2G, 5Y, 2G, 4Y, 2G, 6Y, 2G, K. Y to end.
12th r: P.1(3,5)Y, 1G, 2Y, 1G, 5Y, 9G, 7Y, 1G, 2Y, 1G, 2Y, 1G, 10Y, 9G, 7Y, 1G, 2Y, 1G, 2Y, 1G, 10Y, 9G, 2Y, 1G, 2Y, 1G. P. Y to end.
13th r: K.1(2,4)Y, 2G, 3Y, 10G, 11Y, 1G, 1Y, 1G, 1Y, 1G, 7Y, 10G, 11Y, 1G, 1Y, 1G, 1Y, 1G, 7Y, 10G, 7Y, 2G, K. Y to end.
14th r: P.1(3,5)Y, 1G, 2Y, 1G, 4Y, 11G, 3Y, 2G, 3Y, 1G, 1Y, 1G, 3Y, 2G, 6Y, 11G, 3Y, 2G, 3Y, 1G, 1Y, 1G, 3Y, 2G, 6Y, 11G, 1Y, 1G, 2Y, 1G, P. Y to end.
15th r: K.3(4,6)Y, 2G, 2Y, 10G, 5Y, 6G, 1Y, 1G, 1Y, 6G, 3Y, 10G, 5Y, 6G, 1Y, 1G, 1Y, 6G, 3Y, 10G, 4Y, 2G, K. Y to end.
16th r: P.1(3,5)Y, 1G, 2Y, 1G, 4Y, 4G, 10Y, 2G, 3Y, 1G, 1Y, 1G, 3Y, 2G, 6Y, 4G, 10Y, 2G, 3Y, 1G, 1Y, 1G, 3Y, 2G, 6Y, 4G, 8Y, 1G, 2Y, 1G. P. Y to end.
17th r: K.1(2,4)Y, 2G, 12Y, 5G, 7Y, 1G, 1Y, 1G, 1Y, 1G, 16Y, 5G, 7Y, 1G, 1Y, 1G, 1Y, 1G, 16Y, 5G, 3Y, 2G, K. Y to end.
18th r: P.1(3,5)Y, 1G, 2Y, 1G, 2Y, 3G, 16Y, 1G, 2Y, 1G, 2Y, 1G, 7Y, 3G, 16Y, 1G, 2Y, 1G, 2Y, 1G, 7Y, 3G, 11Y, 1G, 2Y, 1G, P. Y to end.
19th r: K.3(4,6)Y, 2G, 5Y, 3G, 1Y, 2G, 1Y, 1G, 6Y, 2G, 3Y, 1G, 3Y, 2G, 8Y, 3G, 1Y, 2G, 1Y, 1G, 6Y, 2G, 3Y, 1G, 3Y, 2G, 8Y, 3G, 1Y, 2G, 1Y, 1G, 3Y, 2G, K. Y to end.
20th r: P.1(3,5)Y, 1G, 2Y, 1G, 4Y, 1G, 2Y, 1G, 3Y, 1G, 7Y, 2G, 2Y, 3G, 2Y, 2G, 7Y, 1G, 2Y, 1G, 3Y, 1G, 7Y, 2G, 2Y, 3G, 2Y, 2G, 7Y, 1G, 2Y, 1G, 3Y, 1G, 4Y, 1G, 2Y, 1G, P. Y to end.
21st r: K.1(2,4)Y, 2G, 6Y, 1G, 2Y, 1G, 3Y, 1G, 2Y, 1G, 8Y, 3G, 11Y, 1G, 2Y, 1G, 3Y, 1G, 2Y, 1G, 8Y, 3G, 11Y, 1G, 2Y, 1G, 3Y, 1G, 2Y, 1G, 3Y, 2G, K. Y to end.

22nd r: P.1(3,5)Y, 1G, 2Y, 1G, 2Y, 2G, 4Y, 1G, 15Y, 1G, 10Y, 2G, 4Y, 1G, 15Y, 1G, 10Y, 2G, 4Y, 1G, 7Y, 1G, 2Y, 1G, P. Y to end.
23rd r: K3(4,6)Y, 2G, 14Y, 1G, 32Y, 1G, 32Y, 1G, 1Y, 2G, K. Y to end.
24th r: As 6th r.
25th r: As 5th r.
26th r: As 4th r.
27th r: As 3rd r.
28th r: As 2nd r.
29th r: As 1st r.

BOTH TOPS:
Change to No. 3 Ns., and starting with a P. 4., work S.S. until work measures 8(8¼,8½) inches from cast on edge, ending with a K. r.

Next r: Dec. 6(5,5) sts. evenly across the work. (86(90,94) sts. remain). Change to No. 1 Ns., and work 5 rs. of K.2, P.2 rib. Cast off in rib.

RIGHT SHOULDER STRAP:
Using yellow wool and No. 1 Ns., cast on 86(90,94) sts. and work 5 rs. K.2, P.2 rib.
Change to No. 3 Ns. and S.S., and starting with a K.R., work as follows:
1st r: K.43(45,47), K.2 together, K to end.
2nd r: P.42(44,46), P.2 together, P. to end.
3rd r: K.42(44,46), K.2 together, K. to end.
4th r: P.41(43,45), P.2 together, P. to end.
(82(86,90) sts. remain). Change to No. 1 Ns. and work 5 rs. K.2, P.2 rib. Cast off in rib.

LEFT SHOULDER STRAP
Follow the instructions for Right Shoulder Strap, but read P for K. and vice versa, throughout.

TO MAKE UP: Pin out each piece to size and press. Join side seams; press.

Plain Top only: Change to No. 3 Ns. and S.S. and starting with a K. r, continue until work measures $8(8\frac{1}{4},8\frac{1}{2})$ in. from cast-on edge, ending with a K. r.

Fold straps in half and pin each end into position approximately 2 in. in from side seams, with the ends of the straps inside. Catch down the ends of the straps to the first r. of top ribbing. Give final light press.

Zip jacket

MEASUREMENTS:
To fit a child of approximately 5(6, 7) years — chest sizes 23(24, 25) inches. For garment measurements, see diagram.

TENSION:
$7\frac{1}{2}$ sts. and 9 rs. to 1 inch, knitting S.S. on No. 3 Ns.

BACK:
Using WHITE wool and No. 1 Ns., cast on 90(94,98) sts. and work $1\frac{1}{2}$ inches of K.2, P.2 rib, increasing 5 sts. evenly across the work in the last r. 95(99,103) sts. altogether.
Change to No. 3 Ns., and, starting with a K. r., work in S.S. until Back measures 4(4,5) inches from cast-on edge, ending with a P. r.
Work 28 rs. of Fair Isle as follows:
1st r: K.4(6,8)W, *3R, 9W. Repeat from * until 7(9,11) sts. remain. K.3 R, K. W to end.
2nd r: As 1st r, but read P. for K.
3rd r: As 1st r.
4th r: P. W throughout.
5th r: K. W throughout.
6th r: P. 1(3,0)R, 9(9,2)W, *3R, 9W. Repeat from * until 1(3,5) sts. remain. P.1(3,3)R. 3rd size only: P. W to end.
7th r: As 6th r., but read K. for P.
8th r: As 6th r.
9th r: K.5(7,9)W, *1G, 11W. Repeat from * until 6(8,10) sts. remain. K. 1G, K. W to end.
10th r: P.4(6,8)W, * 3G, 9W. Repeat from * until 7(9,11) sts. remain. P. 3G, P. W to end.
11th r: K.3(5,7)W, *5G, 7W. Repeat from * until 8(10,12) sts. remain. K.5G, K.W to end.
12th r: P.2(4,0)W, 7(7,1)G, *5W, 7G. Repeat from * until 2(4,6) sts. remain. P.2(4,5)W.
3rd size only: P.G to end.
13th r: K.1(2,0)W.
3rd size only: K.2G, 3W.
All sizes: *K.4G, 1R, 4G, 3W. Repeat from *until 10(12,14) sts. remain. K.4G, 1R, 4G, 1(3,3)W.
3rd size only: K.G to end.
14th r: P.4(1,3)G.
2nd and 3rd sizes only: P.1W, 4G.
All sizes: *P.3R, 4G, 1W, 4G. Repeat from * until 7(9,11) sts. remain. P.3R, 4G.
2nd and 3rd sizes only: P.1W, P.6 to end.
15th r: K.3(5,7)G, * 5R, 7G. Repeat from * until 8(10,12) sts. remain. K.5R, K.G to end.
16th r: P.2(4,0)G, 7(7,1)R, *5G, 7R. Repeat from * until 2(4,6) sts. remain. P.2(4,5)G.
3rd size only: P. R to end.
17th r: K.1(3,0)G, 9(9,2)R, *3G, 9R. Repeat from * until 1(3,5) sts. remain. K.1(3,3)G.

3rd size only: K.R to end.
18th r: P.1(1,3)R, *1G, 11R. Repeat from * until 0(2,4) sts. remain. P.1G, P.R to end.
**19th r: As 18th r, but read K. for P.
20th r: As 17th r, but read P. for K.
21st r: As 16th r, but read P. for K.
22nd r: As 15th r, but read P. for K.
23rd r: As 14th r, but read P. for K.
24th r: As 13th r, but read P. for K.
25th r: As 12th r, but read P. for K.
26th r: As 11th r, but read P. for K.
27th r: As 10th r, but read P. for K.
28th r: As 9th r, but read P for K.**
Continue in S.S., using WHITE only, until work measures $7\frac{3}{4}(7\frac{3}{4},8\frac{3}{4})$ inches from cast-on edge. Cast off.

FRONTS (2 alike):
Using WHITE wool and No. 1 Ns., cast on 44(46,46) sts. and work $1\frac{1}{2}$ inches of K.2, P.2 rib, increasing 3(3,5) sts. evenly across the work in the last r. 47(49, 51) sts. altogether.
Change to No. 3 Ns. and, starting with a K.R, work in S.S. until Front measures 4(4,5) inches from cast-on edge, ending with a P.R. Work 28 rs. of Fair Isle as follows:
1st r: K.4(5,6)W, *3R, 9W. Repeat from * until 7(8,9) sts. remain. K.3R, K.W to end.
2nd r: As 1st r, but read P. for K.
3rd r: As 1st r.
4th r: P.W. throughout.
5th r: K.W. throughout.
6th r: P.1(2,3)R, *9W, 3R. Repeat from * until 10(11, 12) sts remain. P. P.9W, P.R. to end.
7th r: As 6th R, but read K. for P.
8th r: As 6th R.
9th r: K.5(6,7)W, *1G, 11W. Repeat from * until 6(7,8) sts. remain. K.1G, K.W. to end.
10th r: P.4(5,6)W, *3G, 9W. Repeat from * until 7(8,9) sts. remain. P.3G, P.W to end.
11th r: K.3(4,5)W, *5G, 7W. Repeat from * until 8(9, 10) sts. remain. K.5G, K.W to end.
12th r: P.2(3,4)W, *7G, 5W. Repeat from * until 9(10,11) sts. remain. P.7G, P.W to end.
13th r: K.1(2,3)W,*4G, 1R, 4G, 3W. Repeat from * until 10(11, 12) sts. remain. K.4G, 1R, 4G. K.W to end.
14th r: 2nd and 3rd sizes only P.(1,0)W, (0,1)G, (0,1)W. All sizes: *P.4G, 3R, 4G, 1W.Repeat from *

until 11(12,13) sts. remain. P.4G, 3R, 4G.

2nd and 3rd sizes only: P.1W (0,1)G.
15th r: K.3(4,5)G, *5R, 7G. Repeat from * until 8(9, 10) sts. remain. K.5R, K.G to end.
16th r: P.2(3,4)G, *7R, 5G. Repeat from * until 9(10,11) sts. remain. P.7R, P.G. to end.
17th r: K.1(2,3)G, *9R, 3G. Repeat from * until 10(11, 12) sts. remain. K.9R, K. G to end.
18th r: P.0(1,0)G, 11(11,1)R, *1G, 11R. Repeat from * until 0(1,2) sts. remain. P.0(1,1)G, 0(0,1)R.
Now follow instructions for Back from **to the end.

SLEEVES and YOKE (1 piece):
Using WHITE wool and No. 1 Ns. cast on 42(46,50) sts., and work $1\frac{1}{2}$ inches of K.2, P.2 rib, increasing 7 sts. evenly across the work in the last r. (49(53, 57) sts. altogether.)
Change to No. 3 Ns. and, starting with a K.R., work in S.S. Work 2 rs. Increase 1 st. at both ends of the next and every following 4th (6th, 3rd) r., until the 19th(17th,32nd) increase R. has been worked and there are 87(87,121) sts. Work another 19(5,18) rs. in S.S.
(Work measures 12(13,14) inches from cast on edge.) (Adjust sleeve length at this stage if desired, but always end with a P.r.) Work 28 rs. of Fair Isle as follows:
***1st r: K.0(0,5)W, *3R, 9W. Repeat from * until 3(3,8) sts. remain. K.3R, 0(0,5)W.
2nd r: As 1st R., but read P. for K.
3rd r: As 1st r.
4th r: P.W. throughout.
5th r: K.W. throughout.
6th r: P.6(6,0)W, 3(3,2)R, *9W, 3R. Repeat from * until 6(6,11) sts. remain. P.6(6,9)W, 0(0,2)R.
7th r: As 6th r., but read K. for P.
8th r: As 6th r.
9th r: K.1(1,6)W, *1G, 11W. Repeat from * until 2(2,7) sts. remain. K.1G, K.W. to end.

10th r: P.0(0,5) W, *3G, 9W. Repeat from * until 3(3,8) sts. remain. P.3G, P.W to end.

11th r: K.0(0,4)W, 4(4,5)G, *7W, 5G. Repeat from * until 11 (11,4) sts. remain. K.7 (7,4)W, 4(4,0)G.

12th r: P.0(0,3)W, 5(5,7)G, *5W, 7G. Repeat from * until 10(10,3) sts remain. P.5 (5,3)W, 5(5,0)G.

13th r: K.1(1,0)G.
3rd size only: K.2W, 4G.
All sizes: *K.1R, 4G, 3W, 4G. Repeat from * until 2(2,7) sts remain.
1st and 2nd sizes only: K.1R, 1G.
3rd size only: K.1R, 4G. K.W. to end.

14th r: P.3(3,0)R.
3rd size only: P.1W,4G, 3R.
All sizes: *P.4G, 1W, 4G, 3R. Repeat from * until 0(0,5) sts remain. 3rd size only: P.4G, 1W.

15th r: K.4(4,0)R, 7(7,4)G, *5R, 7G. Repeat from * until 4(4,9) sts remain. K.4 (4,5)R, 0(0,4)G.

16th r: P.5(5,0)R, 5(5,3)G, *7R, 5G. Repeat from * until 5(5,10) sts. remain. P.5 (5,7)R, 0(0,3)G.

17th r: K.6(6,0)R, 3(3,2)G, *9R, 3G. Repeat from * until 6(6,11) sts. remain. K.6(6,9)R, 0(0,2)G.

18th r: P.7(7,0)R, *1G, 11R. Repeat from * until 8(8,1) sts. remain. P.1G, P.R to end.

Now follow instructions for Back from ** to ** ***

Continue in S.S. using WHITE only, and work 5(5,7) rs.

Next r: P.44(44,61) sts, slip the remaining 43(43,60) sts. onto the st. holder. Turn, and work front neckline shaping as follows:

1st r: Cast off 4 sts. at the beginning. K. to end.
2nd r: P.
3rd r: As 1st r.
4th r: P.
5th r: As 1st r.
6th r: P.
7th r: Cast off 3 sts. at the beginning. K. to end.
8th r: P.
9th r: Cast off 2 sts. at the beginning. K. to end.
10th r: P.
11th r: Decrease 1 st at the beginning. K. to end.
12th r: P.
13th r: As 11th r.
14th r: P.
15th r: As 11th r.
24 (24,41) sts. remain. Work a further 4(5,6) rs. Cast off.

With the wrong side of the work facing, pick up the 43(43,60) sts. from the st. holder, rejoin WHITE wool, and starting with a P. r., work 38(40,42) rs. S.S. Slip these sts. back onto the st. holder.

Using No. 3 Ns. and WHITE wool, cast on 24(24,41) sts., and starting with a K. r., work 4(6,6) rs. S.S. *Increase 1 st. at the beginning of the next r. to end. P.1 r. * Repeat from * to * twice more.

Cast on 2 sts. at the beginning of the next r. K. to end. P.1 r.

Cast on 3 sts. at beginning of next r. K. to end. P. 1r.

Cast on 4 sts. at the beginning of the next r. K. to end. P.1 r
Repeat from * to * twice more. 44(44,61) sts. altogether.

With the wrong side of the work facing, pick up the 43(43,60) sts. from the st. holder onto the same N. as the 44(44,61) sts. Rejoin WHITE wool to outer edge of sts. from the st. holder, and starting with a K. r., work 4(4,6) rs. S.S. Now work 28 rs. of Fair Isle, following the instructions from *** to *** Continuing in S.S., using WHITE wool only, work 20(8, 19) rs. If you adjusted the sleeve length previously, remember to make the same adjustment here.

Decrease 1 st. at both ends of the next and every following 4th(6th, 3rd) r., until the 19th(17th, 32nd) decrease r. has been worked, and 49(53,57) sts. remain.

Work 1 r. Decrease 7 sts. evenly across the work in the next r. 42 (46.50) sts remain.

Change to No. 1 Ns., and work 1½ inches of K.2, P.2 rib. Cast off in rib.

NECKBAND

With the wrong side of the yoke facing, and using No. 1 Ns. and WHITE wool, pick up 84(86,88) sts. evenly round the neck edge, and work 2 inches of K.2, P.2 rib. Cast off in rib.

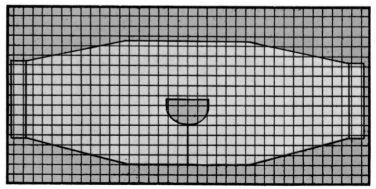

(This chart shows the shape of the yoke and sleeves which are all knitted in one piece.)

Pin out each piece to size and press.

FAIR ISLE CHART

R.S. together, pin and sew fronts and back together along side seams.

R.S. inside, fold yoke and sleeves in half lengthwise. Pin the lower half of jacket in place. Sew along sleeve and yoke seams. Press.

Using White wool and a B crochet hook, work 2 rows of double crochet (see page 78) along both front edges, including neckband edges. Press. Backstitch zipper in place.

Fold neck band in half lengthwise and catch cast-off edge down neatly on inside. Give a final light press.

Fair Isle Mittens

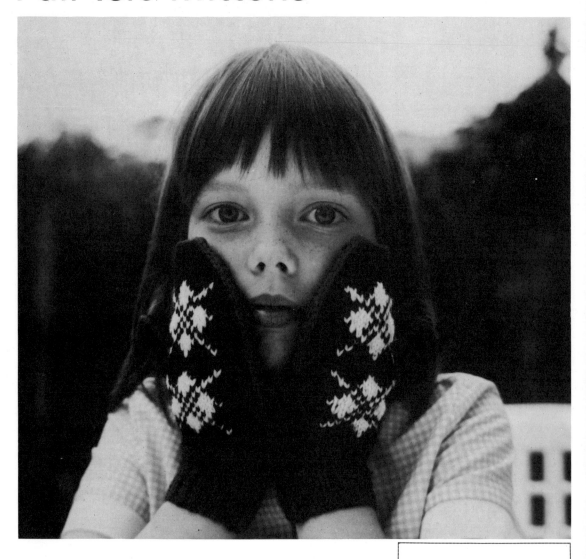

These mittens will fit a child of approximately 6 years old. In our pattern instructions, instead of stipulating row by row to the fair-isle design, we suggest you follow the chart on page 96. This is extremely simple to do — just remember that each square equals 1 stitch, and each horizontal row of square, 1 row. Then just work in stocking stitch following the pattern.

MEASUREMENTS
Completed length (including ribbing): $6\frac{1}{2}(7, 7\frac{1}{2})$ inches.
Completed width across Back: $3\frac{1}{4}$ inches.

TENSION
7 sts. and $8\frac{1}{2}$ rs. to 1 inch, knitting S.S. on No. 3 Ns.

YOU WILL NEED

1 50 grm. Knitting Wool ball in main color (BLACK)
1 50 grm. Knitting Wool ball in first contrast color (RED)
1 50 grm. Knitting Wool ball in second contrast color (WHITE)
A pair of No. 1 and No. 3 knitting needles
A crochet hook size B.

BACKS (2 pieces alike):
Using Red wool and No. 1 Ns. cast on 20 sts. Work 2 inches of K.1, P.1 rib. Change to Black wool and No. 3 Ns. Work in S.S. beginning with a K.r, *K.5 sts. Inc. into next st.* Repeat from * to * twice more (23 sts) altogether.
Continuing in S.S., K.1 (3, 5) rs. Begin working fair isle (see introduction) from chart, and K.24 (26, 28) rs., ending with a P.r.

SHAPE TOP:
Still following fair isle chart at the same time dec. 1st. at both ends of next r. P.1 r. Dec. 1 st. at both ends of the next 4 rs. Cast off 2 sts. at the beginning of the next 2 rs. Cast off the remaining 7 sts.

PALMS (2 pieces alike):
Using Red wool and No. 1 Ns. cast on 16 sts. Work 2 inches of K.1, P.1 rib. Change to Black wool and No. 3 Ns. Beginning with a K.r, * K.4 sts. Inc. into next st.* Repeat from * to * twice more. K.4 sts. (19 sts.). Continuing in S.S., K.25 (29, 33) more rs, ending with a P.r.

SHAPE TOP:
Dec. 1 st. at both ends of next and every following K.r, 5 times altogether. Dec. 1 st. at both ends of next r. Cast off remaining 7 sts.

THUMBS (4 pieces):
FRONTS (2 pieces alike): Using Black wool and No. 3 Ns., cast on 2 sts. Working in S.S., K.1 r. Inc. 1 st. at the end of the next and every following P.r, 5 times (7 sts.). Work 7 (9, 11) rs. Dec. 1 st. at both ends of the next 2 rs. P.1 r. Dec. 1 st. at beginning of the next r. Cast off remaining 2 sts.

BACKS (2 pieces alike): Work as for Fronts, but reverse shaping by beginning with a P.r, and then read K. for P. and vice versa.

Above are all knitted pieces that make up the mittens. Black dots indicate places for pinning them out.

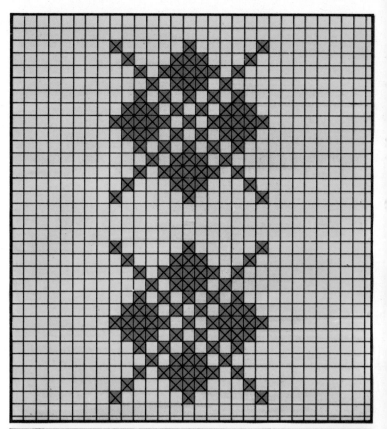

TO MAKE UP

Pin out each piece to size and press as given in Notes. Sew diagonally shaped end of each Thumb piece to appropriate Back and Palm, with lower edge approximately $\frac{3}{4}$ in. above top of ribbing.

Place each Back and Palm together and using Red wool and a size B crochet hook, join the pieces together by working 1 r. of double crochet sts. all around. Give a final light press.